Victorian
DECORATIVE
PAINTING

Victorian DECORATIVE PAINTING

with Brenda Stewart, CDA

NORTH LIGHT BOOKS
CINCINNATI, OHIO
www.nlbooks.com

About the Author

Brenda Stewart has been painting since she was a child. Though her education and training are in fine art, she is best known for her contribution to the field of decorative painting.

Brenda began teaching classes locally in 1971 and has taught her techniques at seminars and conventions throughout the United States and internationally since 1979. She is the author of fifteen books and four videos, and her work has been published in many leading painting magazines. Brenda received her Certified Decorative Artist award in 1979. She has been an active member of the Society of Decorative Painters, serving on committees, as board member at large and as president.

For fifteen years, Brenda and her husband, Robert, lived in a restored 1886 plantation cottage in Louisiana, where they operated a retail shop and seminar studio. Their new home and studio facility is located in Williamsburg, Virginia.

Brenda's earlier career was divided between her shared loves of art and music: She has taught both choral music and piano. A natural teacher, she is most happy when instructing. She possesses the rare ability to relate to each individual student, and to encourage them to stretch to the limits of their abilities.

Brenda and Robert have two married daughters and four grandchildren. Her free time is busy with children, grandchildren, church activities, music, antiquing and travel. Over the past year, building a new home has given Brenda the opportunity to pursue a growing interest in architectural and environmental design.

Other fine North Light Books are available from your local bookstore, art supply store or direct from the publisher.

04 03 02 01 00   5 4 3 2 1

Library of Congress Cataloging-in-Publication Data

Stewart, Brenda
    Victorian decorative painting with Brenda Stewart, CDA.
        p.   cm.
    Includes index.
    ISBN 0-89134-936-7 (alk. paper)
    1. Acrylic painting—Technique. 2. Decoration and ornament—Victorian style. 3. Painted woodwork. 4. China painting.
    I. Title.
TT385.S75   1999
745.7'23—dc21   99-31222
                                                       CIP

Editor: Jennifer Long
Production Editor: Christine Doyle
Production Coordinator: Kristen Heller
Cover Designer: Wendy Dunning
Interior Designer: Sandy Conopeotis Kent

Dedication

This book is dedicated to my deceased father, who put pencil and paint brush in my hands at age seven. Also, to my husband, Robert, who has supported me in the pursuit of every dream; to my girls and their families, who have always understood when Mom had deadlines to meet; and to my friends and students who have supplied me with both inspiration and drive.

Acknowledgments

This book would never have come into being without the many teachers and artists who have shared with me over my long artistic journey. Their patience and encouragement are greatly appreciated.

I would also like to thank all the folks at North Light Books, especially my editor, Jennifer Long. Her patience and assistance through a difficult year have made it possible to complete this book.

To the kind people at Winsor & Newton Col-Art Americas and DecoArt, I thank you for your years of support.

And I acknowledge, once again, the many contributions of my husband, Robert, and thank God, the source of my talent and all things beautiful.

Table of Contents

Introduction

Over the years, I have based my publishing and teaching selections on variety: variety of subject matter, variety of mediums and variety of surfaces. I have chosen some of my favorite subjects, mediums and surfaces for the projects in this book. Included are paintings on wood, porcelain and paper, done in acrylics, alkyds and watercolors. The subjects range from a Santa and an angel to florals and still lifes.

Variety is necessary for building skills as an artist and for fostering growth and development of creativity. It is not necessary to like everything an artist does in order to learn from her. When studying with an artist or working from her books, you may pick up only one or two usable techniques. But each experience is valuable to the overall growth and learning process. Art is an experiential process; every different encounter contributes to the overall education of an artist.

The first step in painting from any book is to read carefully and study each illustration. I sometimes read and study a book, photographic reference or sketch many times before attempting to put the information to work in an actual painting. A watercolor instructor I studied with as a young person always told the class to "Observe three times, think twice and paint once." That adage has become ingrained in my painting philosophy. Being a very impatient, enthusiastic person, however, I sometimes forget to put this practice to use. At those times, I often experience mistakes and frustrations in my painting.

Independent painting is as important as classroom instruction to the growth of an artist. These two experiences offer very different learning opportunities. Working in class provides basic skills and knowledge by both visual and verbal means. It should be an environment where help and correction are available. Publications offer information in a totally visual format, to be read and observed. New information and techniques are assimilated, but a different type of growth is experienced as one executes the painting independently. A further growth step is taken when an artist utilizes the sum of all he or she has learned and executes an original work.

It is my hope that you will find projects and information in this book to stretch your techniques, knowledge and scope of experience. It is my intention to teach skills and impart knowledge that will enable you to execute not only these proscribed projects, but many independently accomplished works.

Materials

Paints and Mediums

Always purchase the best quality paints possible. Top-quality paints will make a difference in the appearance of the completed painting. I prefer to work with artist-grade products—the pigment is richer and I can achieve a given result with less work. There are less-expensive products available, but they contain less pigment, so you get less for your money. Most of my techniques use very small amounts of paint. I start with a limited palette of colors; from these I can make many color mixtures. If you prefer working the acrylic projects with bottled acrylic paints, choose the best ones available.

Winsor & Newton Finity Artists' Acrylics
I used Finity acrylics to paint the acrylic designs in this book. I dilute these with the Flow Improver mix (see page 18), and often use them in semitransparent layers. They give a beautiful depth and brilliance. You will need eleven colors to paint the projects in this book: Burnt Umber, Cadmium Yellow Medium, Dioxazine Purple, Gold Ochre, Naphthol Red Medium, Naples Yellow, Phthalo Blue Red Shade, Red Iron Oxide, Renaissance Gold, Silver and Titanium White.

Winsor & Newton Griffin Alkyds
I used Griffin alkyds to paint the two alkyd projects, the "Victorian Rose Tray" and "Vintage Violets." I also used them to antique the "Magnolia Tray" project. Alkyds have a beautiful natural luminosity. I used a very limited palette for the projects in this book: Alizarin Crimson, Burnt Umber, Cadmium Yellow Light, Dioxazine Purple, Naples Yellow Hue, Phthalo Blue and Titanium White.

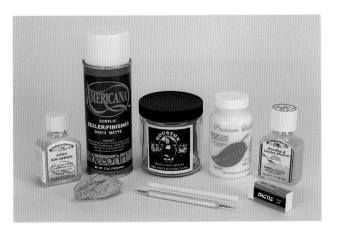

Winsor & Newton Artists' Oils
I use these oils occasionally with my alkyds if I need a color that isn't available in the alkyd line. Renaissance Gold is the only oil paint needed for this book.

Winsor & Newton Artists' Water Colours
These watercolors are of the highest quality available today. They produce wonderful brilliance and clarity of tone and have very rich pigmentation. I prefer the tube paints rather than pans. The colors called for in this book are Burnt Umber, Cadmium Yellow Pale, Gold Ochre, Oxide of Chromium, Permanent Alizarin Crimson, Sepia and Winsor Blue Red Shade.

Winsor & Newton Designers' Gouache
I sometimes call for gouache in my watercolor instructions. On the rare occasion when I use white in a watercolor painting, I use the Bleedproof White gouache. I use this white to add a bit of sparkle or highlight in an area too small to have saved the white of the paper, or where I do not wish to use a masking fluid.

DecoArt Americana Acrylics
I use DecoArt Americana bottled acrylics to basecoat the surfaces prior to painting the designs. They have a wide color range and are a nice consistency for our painting purposes. They also possess very strong pigment. To prepare the projects in this book you will need Black Plum DA172, Desert Sand DA7, French Mocha DA188, Grey Sky DA111, Light Buttermilk DA164, Midnite Green DA84, TitaniumWhite DA1 and Warm Neutral DA90.

Mediums
To improve the flow and consistency of my paint and aid in blending, I use Winsor & Newton Acrylic Flow Improver and Winsor & Newton Blending & Glazing Medium.

Brushes

There are many wonderful brushes on the market, bearing many different brand names. No one can try them all. Because students always want to know which "magic brush" the teacher uses, I will list those I use most:

Winsor & Newton Synthetics
- Series 500 no. 4 and no. 6 flats
- Series 545 ¼-inch (6mm) and ½-inch (12mm) square combs
- Series 550 no. 2 and no. 4 filberts
- Series 555 ½-inch (12mm) oval comb
- Series 560 ⅛-inch (3mm), ¼-inch (6mm), ⅜-inch (10mm), ½-inch (12mm), ¾-inch (19mm) and 1-inch (25mm) angles
- Series 565 1-inch (25mm) flat
- Series 575 ½-inch (12mm) and 1-inch (25mm) oval filbert mops
- Series 580 ⅛-inch (3mm) one-stroke lettering

Winsor & Newton Series 965, 1-inch (25mm) or 1½-inch (38mm) short-handled flat synthetic/natural hair blend wash brush

Winsor & Newton Sables
- Series 7 no. 0 or no. 1 Kolinsky sable round
- Series 700 no. 0 and no. 2 flats
- Series 720 no. 6 or no. 8 and no. 10 or no. 12 red sable rounds
- Series 740 no. 1 and no. 10 red sable liner and round
- Series 760 ⅛-inch (3mm), ¼-inch (6mm), ⅜-inch (10mm), ½-inch (12mm) and ¾-inch (19mm) angles

Mop Brushes
- Winsor & Newton Series 240 no. 1 and no. 2 white mops
- Loew Cornell Mini and Detail mops

Winsor & Newton Series 5977 no. 1 or no. 3 hog bristle fan

> ### ✧ Tip ✧
> I have switched almost entirely to angled brushes for laying in color, side loading, shading, etc. I much prefer them to flats, but still use some flats for special purposes. ✧

Caring for Your Brushes

I am sometimes appalled at the condition of the brushes I see being used by students. Regardless of brand, brushes are one of a painter's major expenses. It is imperative that they be in top condition, so, please, take care of them!

Sables (or synthetics used for oils or alkyds)

1. After each painting session, remove excess paint using a soft paper towel and synthetic turpentine or brush cleaning fluid.
2. Using Artgel, clean the brushes in the palm of your hand or gently against your palette until all traces of color disappear. I do not like to use soap or soap-based products for normal cleanup.
3. When the brush is thoroughly clean, leave a little of the Artgel in the bristles and smooth them into their natural shape. Store the brushes in a covered container. Be certain the bristles are not leaning on the sides of the container or being bent.
4. Rinse the brushes in clean turpentine to remove the Artgel prior to your next painting session.

Synthetics (used for acrylics)

It is important to clean acrylic brushes thoroughly after each painting session. Small brushes and liners may also need to be cleaned several times during a painting period.

1. Pour a little alcohol into a flat lid or saucer.
2. Use a toothbrush to brush gently from the ferrule to the top of the bristle. Give extra attention to the hair right at the ferrule—this is where the acrylic paint builds up. This method has conquered the acrylic brush "bushies" for me. You will find it an excellent way to prolong the life of large synthetics used to apply basecoats and waterbase varnish.
3. After a thorough cleaning, rinse the brush in clean water and reshape with a bit of Artgel. Store the brushes in a covered container, making sure the bristles are not leaning on the sides of the container or being bent.
4. Prior to another painting session, rinse brushes in clean water to remove Artgel.

Getting Started

Preparing and Finishing Your Surface

Preparing Wood

1. Fill any holes with wood filler, following the manufacturer's directions. Allow to dry. Sand the piece with Flex-I-Grit medium-fine sanding film and wipe clean with a tack cloth.
2. Seal with a penetrating wood sealer. Allow to dry as directed.
3. Sand again lightly with the fine sanding film. Wipe with the tack cloth.
4. The wood is now ready to be painted with acrylic washes or solid basecoating.

Basecoating With Acrylics

1. Apply the basecoat in several even, thin coats. Use as large a brush as possible for each given area. Dampen the surface prior to each coat to eliminate overlap lines. If the acrylic paint used for the basecoating is too thick to flow well, thin it with water to obtain a flowing consistency. Allow each coat to dry well before applying another. As long as the surface feels cool to the touch, it is not thoroughly dry.
2. Continue to apply thin, even coats until you have a satisfactory painting surface. After the final coat, rub lightly with a small piece of Scuff Rite pad or Flex-I-Grit extra-fine finishing film. Wipe with a tack cloth.
3. If the painting is to be done in oils or alkyds and the basecoat does not contain sealer, or if the basecoat has a chalky, "draggy" feeling, spray lightly with several coats of DecoArt Americana matte acrylic spray.

Basecoating With Acrylic Washes

1. Dampen each area prior to applying the wash. This will eliminate overlap lines in your washes and enable you to obtain a more even value in the wash.
2. Keep a clean, damp brush handy while you work to redampen areas that dry before you are able to apply the wash to them. When this happens, dampen the unwashed area and work back to where the wash color stopped. The damp brush is also useful to make corrections in the washes where color is too heavy, streaky or the strokes are not straight.
3. Use as large a brush as possible for applying washes. The strokes should be long and smooth. The fewer strokes in an area, the better.
4. Several light washes are preferable to applying the color too heavily and too quickly.
5. Be certain each wash is thoroughly dry before applying another.
6. If the wood grain is raised by the washes, skim lightly over the final coat with a small piece of Scuff Rite pad or Flex-I-Grit extra-fine finishing film. Wipe with a tack cloth.

Staining Wood

1. Thin oil color to the desired consistency (thinner color creates a lighter stain) with odorless turpentine or paint thinner. You may also use a commercial stain.
2. Apply with a soft, lint-free cloth or a brush. Allow to set up briefly.
3. Wipe with a soft, lint-free cloth until you achieve the desired value.
4. Allow to dry. Spray with several light coats of DecoArt Americana matte acrylic spray if painting with oils or alkyds.

Preparing Porcelain

1. Most porcelain now available needs no preparation other than washing and drying. Use a mild dishwashing liquid for washing. Rinse well and dry thoroughly.
2. If the porcelain has any rough spots, sand with Flex-I-Grit fine or extra-fine finishing film and wipe before washing.
3. If the porcelain is of poor quality or is extremely rough, wash, then give it several light coats of DecoArt Americana matte acrylic spray.

Preparing Watercolor Paper

Stretching watercolor paper reduces buckling or curling as you paint. If you choose, you may work on paper that has not been stretched. This is applicable to paintings where large background areas will not receive excessive wetting. A framer can put the painting in a mounting press to remove any buckling that occurs. Specify that the paintings are not to be vacuum mounted.

1. If paper is to be stretched for your project, soak it in a clean container filled with clean water. Clean hands and clean work surfaces are a must when working with watercolor paper.
2. Remove paper from the water and staple to a clean board. Begin stapling from the center of each edge and work out to the corners. You may also use Scotch brand tape no. 810 to attach the paper to the board.
3. If the paper is wet, allow it to dry before you begin the painting.
4. After the painting is complete, allow the paper to dry thoroughly, then remove from the board.

Tracing and Transferring the Pattern

1. Make an accurate tracing of the pattern on tracing paper. The smaller the pattern, the more accurate you must be. I prefer a good technical pen or a Pigma Micron pen for making my tracing paper drawings.
2. Position the tracing on the surface and tape in place. Slide a piece of gray or steno white graphite paper underneath.
3. Using a fine-point stylus, lightly go over the pattern lines, transferring them to the surface. Transfer only the most necessary lines. The lines should be fine, but clearly visible.

To transfer a pattern to watercolor paper, place the watercolor paper over a lightbox and position the pattern underneath. (If you don't have a lightbox, improvise by placing a lamp under a glass-topped table, or tape the paper and pattern to a sunlit window.) Use a fine-point pencil to transfer the lines. You can also cover the back of another sheet of tracing paper with graphite using a soft lead pencil and transfer as directed in steps one through three. Apply a minimum of lines to watercolor paper.

Antiquing

1. Seal the background to be antiqued with matte acrylic spray or one coat of finish varnish. I seldom apply antiquing until after the painting is completed, so I use the finish varnish.
2. With a piece of lint-free towel, rub a scant coating of Winsor & Newton Blending & Glazing Medium—or a mixture of equal parts linseed oil and odorless turpentine—on the surface to be antiqued.

3. With a dry brush, apply oil or alkyd color; I often use a mixture from the project palette. (An alternate method is to mix the medium directly into the oil or alkyd paint, apply it to the surface, and then continue with the following steps.)
4. Wipe off excess with a piece of lint-free towel. Soften with a large mop brush. Lift off any areas that need to be lightened with a small pad of lint-free towel. Mop again to remove wipe marks and do the final softening.
5. Allow to dry. Spray with DecoArt Americana matte acrylic spray to set, or continue with coats of finish varnish.

Spattering

1. Thin the paint with the appropriate solvent (water for acrylics or watercolors; Winsor & Newton Blending & Glazing Medium, odorless turpentine or paint thinner for oils or alkyds). I often use a color mixture from the painting for spattering.
2. Load a medium to large fan brush with the soupy paint. Rake a small palette knife across the width of the brush. Test this technique on a practice surface until you have the correct paint load, consistency and control.
3. Allow to dry, then varnish. If you're spattering with oils or alkyds, spray with DecoArt Americana matte acrylic spray to set the spatters, then continue with coats of finish varnish.

Finishing Wooden Surfaces

1. Wipe the surface, stirring tool and brush with a tack cloth before each coat.
2. Apply the varnish evenly, using a large, flat, synthetic brush. This brush should be used solely for varnishing purposes. Watch for drips and runs.
3. Allow to dry as directed.
4. Repeat the above steps as many times as you desire. After the third coat, wet sand very lightly with Flex-I-Grit extra-fine finishing film. Wipe the surface dry, then wipe it with the tack cloth. A minimum of four coats are needed for a well-protected painting. Eight to ten coats give an added depth to the painting.
5. Allow the final coat to cure for several days. Apply a coat of finishing wax with a soft cloth or very fine steel wool. Wipe with a soft cloth. If the painted piece is handled frequently or heavily used, apply a fresh coat of wax every six to twelve months.

Finishing Porcelain Surfaces

1. When the painting is complete and thoroughly dry, wipe the piece with a clean tack cloth.
2. Apply eight to ten coats of Blair Satin Tole to the piece. Before each coat, shake the can thoroughly. When spraying, hold the can twelve to fifteen inches from the surface. Do not apply spray varnish indoors, and wear a mask while spraying. Never apply in periods of high humidity, and do not rush coats—allow each to dry thoroughly before applying the next. If clouding occurs, it will disappear with successive coats.

> ### ☙ Tip ❧
>
> *For some acrylic or watercolor paintings, I dampen the surface prior to spattering. This gives a softened effect to the spatters. Many times I add spattering while the surface is damp, then continue when the surface is dry for sharper spatters. ☙*

Painting With Acrylics

After you've completed all preparation and patterning steps as instructed previously, begin your painting by basecoating each area of the design with one of three methods: a solid base, a solid wash base or a side-loaded base.

- A solid base will produce solid, opaque color. More than one coat is usually needed to obtain an even value. The paint must be thinned with water just enough to obtain a flowing consistency and must be evenly loaded into the brush.
- A solid wash base will produce an even, overall wash of color, but will be transparent or semi-transparent. The paint must be thinned with water to a certain value, specified by the instructions. It is even more important for the color to be loaded evenly in the brush for the solid wash basecoat. Uneven color in the brush will result in a streaky, uneven appearance in your basecoat.
- A side-loaded base produces a basecoat with value gradations. Highlight areas of the ground color will often be left showing. For this method of basing, the brush is side loaded with color, then softened on the palette. Blend until a nice gradation of color is achieved.

Next, apply the tints and highlights to all areas. They are normally applied using a wet-on-wet technique and are often side loaded into the brush. Detail and linework complete the painting. Use the deepest shading color for the detail and linework unless otherwise specified.

ACRYLIC MEDIUMS

- Dilute Winsor & Newton Acrylic Flow Improver to a ratio of one part Flow Improver to twenty parts water. Mix this diluted Flow Improver into each pure tube color on the palette prior to making mixtures for each project. Mix the paint to the consistency of soupy sour cream.
- Water is the only medium used during the actual painting of the project.

Solid Base
Select a brush of the appropriate size for the area to be painted. Load with acrylic paint that has been thinned just enough to obtain a flowing consistency. Apply pressure as you load and blend the paint evenly into the brush. With as few strokes as possible, cover the area to be painted with the first basecoat. Allow the first coat to dry thoroughly, then repeat the basecoating as many times as necessary to obtain smooth, even, solid color. If the area to be basecoated is large, predampen the surface with water. This will give a smoother, ridge-free basecoat.

Solid Wash Base
Thin acrylic paint with water to the value of wash called for in the project instructions. (This leaf is a medium-value wash.) Load an appropriately sized brush with the thinned paint. It is imperative that you spend adequate time loading the wash into the brush on the palette. The wash must be an even value throughout the brush. Dampen the area with clear water prior to applying the wash. With as few strokes as possible, apply an even wash to the entire area. If another coat is needed to obtain a deeper or more even value, allow the first wash to dry and repeat the above steps.

Side-Loaded Base

Tip one corner of an appropriately sized brush into the base-coat color. Move to another spot on the palette and stroke the brush back and forth to blend the paint into both the front and back of the brush. Blend until a gradation of color is obtained in the brush. If you need to widen the area of the side load, walk back into the paint side of the blending area as you blend the color into the brush. If the load is the right width in the brush, blend the brush, moving the brush away from the paint side of the blending area—good side loading is done on the palette. When the brush is properly loaded, dampen the area to be painted with clear water. Turn the color side of the brush toward the stronger portions of the area and apply the basecoat, walking it out as needed. In a complex area, you may not obtain all basecoating with one step. Do a portion, allow it to dry, then return to the area to add different sections of basecoating to deepen that which has already been applied or to expand an area in size.

Wet-on-Wet Techniques

- Dampening each area with clear water prior to basing, shading or adding highlights allows you to paint in acrylics without developing overlap lines or lines on blending edges. Do not dampen prior to detail or linework unless softening is desired.

- Always work with as large a brush as possible in each area. This will enable you to achieve each step more quickly, with a minimum of brush-strokes.

- Work each step quickly. As an area begins to set up, stop work. Allow the step to dry before continuing to paint in the area.

- To achieve the desired strength of value changes within an area, it may require repetitive overpaintings.

- Each deeper value of shading should be contained within the previously painted area and should cover less area than the previous application of color. Place the deepest shading within triangles and crescents. Likewise, each lighter value will build within the previous light value. Work up the scale of values gradually, being careful not to "jump" values.

Painting With Alkyds

Alkyds are named for the binder (or glue) used to hold the powdered pigment together. The binder in alkyds is an alkyd resin, derived from plants. The resin binder produces a paint that is highly adhesive, tough, flexible and resistant to solvents when dry. While wet, alkyds are soluble in turpentine or petroleum solvent. They are compatible with oils and may be used with the same brushes, solvents, etc. I have found alkyds to offer the following advantages:

- Alkyds dry more quickly than oils, yet slower than acrylics. They remain moist and workable long enough for use of familiar oil painting application and blending techniques, but are dry enough within hours to allow for overpainting and glazing. When using oils, especially in humid areas, it may be days before glazing can be done.
- Drying time of colors is uniform: Cadmium Red dries as quickly as Burnt Umber.
- Because alkyds set up so rapidly, darker shadows, highlights, tints, etc. may be added more quickly and with greater ease.
- Alkyds have a great brilliance and luminosity. There is more "life" to the dry color than that of an unvarnished oil paint. This is another plus for use with the porcelain techniques, as this is the only surface on which I do not use multiple coats of brush-on varnish.
- Alkyds work beautifully for strokework borders and trims. The large understroke sets up quickly and the liner strokework eases right over it. And within a few hours, the border is dry enough to pat on the soft background colors.

Painting on Porcelain Bisque or Vellum-Coated China Pieces

When painting porcelain, you will sometimes complete all steps in one stage. More often though, you will glaze or overpaint to enhance the painting. Use scant amounts of alkyd paint on bisque—just enough to tint the surface. The porcelain technique may also be used for painting on wood or canvas prepared with an off-white or light acrylic background.

1. Apply a very scant amount of Winsor & Newton Blending & Glazing Medium to the area to be painted. Apply this medium with a brush set aside for this purpose. Paint is drybrushed onto the porcelain surface; you don't want to use a brush wet with medium for any of the painting steps.

✑ Tip ✑

Drying time is relative to the amount of paint used. On porcelain, where very thin layers of paint are used, three or four overpaintings may be done in one day (even using Winsor & Newton Blending & Glazing Medium or a mix of linseed oil and odorless turpentine to dress the surface). A thickly painted canvas would require more drying time. ✑

✑ Tip ✑

The Winsor & Newton Blending & Glazing Medium contains damar varnish. If you are bothered by the odor of the varnish, you may substitute a mixture of equal portions of linseed oil and odorless turpentine or paint thinner for the Blending & Glazing Medium. ✑

---

2. Using a dry brush, basecoat the area as instructed in the project, using an angle brush or shorthaired flat brush. (The short bristle length is important because you will be using a small amount of paint, stretched on the surface, and the shorter-haired brushes will accomplish this more easily.) Use as large a brush as you can comfortably handle in an area. Apply enough paint to cover and obtain good color, without having excess paint on the surface.

   When more than one color is used, wipe the brush after applying colors, then blend the color breaks softly, stroking the brush parallel to the color breaks. Wipe the brush often. Blend until values are graded. When one color is used for basecoating, wipe the brush after the application is complete, then buff/blend to smooth and remove excess paint.

3. Apply the shading values next. Use a side-loaded angle brush. Load the shading into the longer side of the brush. Wipe the brush and blend as needed. Blending strokes should be parallel to the color break. Blend until values are graded.

━ *Tip* ━

A deeper shading may be added in the first or second painting. When adding deeper shading, use a side-loaded brush. Apply these deeper values to triangular areas where objects overlap, or to deeper recesses of shadow points. Each darker value stays within the previous value, covering less area. ━

4. Apply the tints next. These may be applied in the first painting or in an overpainting. They are usually added to middle-value areas, overlapping into the edges of shaded and lighter areas. They are sometimes applied on the edges of an object, such as leaf edges. Apply the tints very softly with a side-loaded brush. Wipe the brush and blend until tints are graded into the object.

━ *Tip* ━

Tints should not appear "spotty" or be so strong as to draw the eye. They should be soft and subtle. ━

5. Lighter values and highlights are added next. Apply these with a side-loaded brush. After applying, wipe the brush and blend color breaks. Lighter values build within the previously applied value, with the lighter value occupying less space.

6. Detail or linework may be added in the first painting or in an overpainting. When applied in the first painting, it is meant to be softer and more subdued than when added on a dry ground. Thin the paint with Blending & Glazing Medium or turpentine. The brush should be well loaded, with no lumps or globs of paint on the brush. Push the paint into the bristles and roll to a point. Many times linework is softened with a mop after allowing a brief setup time.

7. I seldom complete an alkyd painting without one or a series of overpaintings. Overpainting is done after the first or previous painting is thoroughly dry. These overpainting steps are used throughout the project to enhance color, accent darks and brighten highlights. The painting can be refined to an unlimited degree with overpainting. To overpaint, first apply a scant amount of Blending & Glazing Medium to the surface. Buff gently with a dry brush to remove excess medium. Then apply color with a dry, side-loaded brush. Blend the paint into the wet, glazed background.

━ *Tip* ━

Use very small amounts of paint when glazing. Far less is required than when doing the first painting. Be very cautious with light colors. Do not "jump" values. When glazing, lights and highlights will not require as light a value as in the initial painting. ━

Painting With Watercolors

To offer you a little more variety, I've included one watercolor project in this book: "Flow Blue and Daffodils." If you've never painted in watercolor before, consider the project, as well as these general instructions, as an introduction to watercolor. I believe techniques used with watercolor vary more from artist to artist than techniques in any other medium. Because there are so many different techniques that may be used with watercolor, there is great opportunity for personal interpretation. Wonderful things "happen" on the surface, perhaps a bit differently each time you paint. Building experience in the medium is very important as you learn what effects you can achieve and what you prefer. Relax, be loose and allow the painting to happen for you!

Palette

I prefer a rectangular palette with many paint wells around the edges. There is normally a large central mixing area, or perhaps several smaller mixing wells and one larger one. The back side of the 12″ × 16″ (30cm × 41cm) Sta-Wet acrylic palette is an excellent watercolor palette, and one that many students already have among their supplies.

Brushes

We all have our favorite brushes. When I first began painting in watercolor, sable brushes were used almost entirely. Now, as the cost of sable has skyrocketed, many different types of brushes are used. Whatever bristle type you start with—sable, synthetic or a combination bristle—I believe you become accustomed to that particular brush and to how much moisture it carries. I now work with a mix of brushes, including Kolinsky sable, synthetic and a blend of synthetic and natural hair. I still prefer sable rounds and liners above all, and if you are going to splurge on one brush, let it be an excellent quality large round sable.

Paints

Squeeze the paint out into individual palette slots. I set up my palette in the following order, beginning on the left and working to the right: yellows, reds,

> ### ❦ Tip ❦
> If you are right-handed, work with your water, paper towels and brushes to your right. Your paper should be directly in front of you, with the palette next to it on the right. A large, clean kitchen sponge is excellent to have on hand for blotting water from your brush. I use this in addition to a roll of paper towels cut in half or a thick pad of paper towels. When the sponge becomes too moist, squeeze it out. When the paper towels are too wet, change sides of the roll or begin with another pad of towels. The surface that you use for blotting must be very absorbent. ❦

violets, blues, greens, grays and blacks. I place each brown near its predominant hue; for example, a golden brown would be placed with the yellows, a brown with a red overtone goes with the reds, and neutral browns go toward the black end of the palette. The specific order is not as important as long as you are consistent with your setup and always know where colors are located. Until you are familiar with the colors, you may identify them by marking the edges of your palette.

Techniques and Terms

Dry Ground—When the instructions tell you to work on a dry ground, this means that the paper should be thoroughly dry. It will not be cool to the touch.

Slightly Damp Ground—Sometimes you want an area to soften only slightly, and in a more controlled manner. This is achieved by "skimming" the surface of the paper with a damp, blotted brush. Work less area at a time than when working on a damp ground.

Painting Wet-on-Wet
1. Thoroughly wet the area to be painted. Work the moisture into the paper. The paper has less glisten as the moisture works into the paper. You will learn from experience when the paper is at the correct stage for a given effect.
2. Drop in a color or colors. Values of color are always given in the instructions. Until you learn to recognize the correct load the brush should carry for a given result, always blot the loaded brush before applying it to the painting.

3. If time permits, stronger values may be dropped in while the painting is in the process of drying. Always blot the brush before painting in a partially dry or damp surface. The surface will reach a point at which it is too dry for the added values to soften. If this happens, and the color will not soften, gently blend the edges of the color with a very damp, dry-blotted brush.

Introducing Water to an Area—Sometimes, while working a very large area with the wet-on-wet technique, the paper will dry before you are able to complete a step. This happens to me more frequently in large background or sky areas. When this occurs, pick up water in a large brush and blot it. Apply the water to an area beyond where you are working and gradually work back toward the area where you've applied paint.

Tickling the Edges of a Color—This technique is used when color has been dropped on dry ground, but you wish to blend or soften it into the surrounding area. You may then tickle the blending edges with a damp, blotted brush. Different brushes are used for different areas and effects. Some of my favorites are large filberts (sometimes referred to as oval mops), a round brush or the tip of an angle or flat. When you tickle an edge, approach from beyond the applied color, touch just the color edge and pull it out.

Occasionally, a color edge will set before you have had time to soften it. Before attempting a more drastic scrubbing out of color, try applying fresh pigment to the line. Many times this will reactivate the underlying pigment, allowing it to soften quite easily.

Blending Edges of Color—This may be accomplished by tickling as described above, or by straddling a color line with a flat wash or angle brush and walking out to grade the color.

Changing Values—The value of watercolor is changed by using more or less water. A strong value would be paint to which just enough water has been added to obtain a flowing consistency. A medium value would have more water, a light value even more, and a pale value wash the most water. One of the things you will constantly be testing is your color values.

Changing Hues—Hues will be changed by mixing colors together on the palette or by glazing color over color on the painting.

Lifting Color—Lifting of color is useful if you have a blossom or backwash line, a hard line in an undesirable area, or simply have too dark a color that needs to be lightened. To lift, apply water to the area and allow it to penetrate the surface of the paper. Using a soft, short-bristled synthetic brush, gently scrub the area to loosen the pigment. Then blot with a tissue. This may be repeated as many times as necessary.

Use of White Gouache or Opaque White—I sometimes use Winsor & Newton Designers' Gouache Bleedproof White to make corrections that cannot be handled by lifting color. It may be used to lighten or even paint out a small area that you cannot correct. You may need to apply the color several times to correct stubborn areas. If working in a softer background area, soften the edges of the applied white into the background colors. If it appears too white or chalky, allow it to dry and glaze surrounding colors very transparently and gently over it.

I also use the Bleedproof White on occasion to highlight an area. In the watercolor project in this book, it was used to apply highlights to the pitcher, because I wanted a softer shine area than would be achieved with masking. I sometimes also use it to highlight an edge of a flower petal or add to a tiny stamen or other similar small area, or to add highlights on small faces.

Santa Plate

Santas are a favorite subject of many decorative painters. Because so many are painted, taught and sold, on occasion it's nice to paint one in nontraditional colors. This particular Santa, painted in mauves and grayed greens, is a softer approach to the normal holiday red and green.

This project uses most of the basic acrylic techniques discussed in the previous section. It incorporates both solid wash and side-loaded basecoating, and the background color is used as the light value in several areas. This project also provides an excellent opportunity to practice your fine linework. This design enables you to put all these techniques to work in a simple, unintimidating composition.

Santa may be painted on many different surfaces. He would be lovely on a box, with the strokework border trim painted on the sides. I have painted a version of him in alkyds on a porcelain pitcher. Whatever surface you choose, I hope you enjoy the painting experience.

MATERIALS

Palette

Winsor & Newton Finity Artists' Acrylics

- Burnt Umber
- Dioxazine Purple
- Naphthol Red Medium
- Naples Yellow
- Phthalo Blue Red Shade
- Red Iron Oxide
- Titanium White

DecoArt Americana Acrylic Paints

- Titanium White DA1
- Warm Neutral DA90

Surface

This 12-inch (30cm) double-bead plate is available from Brenda Stewart by Design, 228 Yorkshire Dr., Williamsburg, VA 23185; phone (757) 564-7093.

Winsor & Newton Brushes

- Series 7 no. 0 Kolinsky sable round
- Series 500 no. 6 flat
- Series 550 no. 8 synthetic filbert
- Series 560 ⅛-inch (3mm), ¼-inch (6mm), ⅜-inch (10mm), ½-inch (12mm) and ¾-inch (19mm) synthetic angles
- Series 740 no. 1 red sable liner

Medium

Winsor & Newton Acrylic Flow Improver, diluted mix

This pattern may be hand-traced or photocopied for personal use only. Shown at full size.

Preparation

Sand the plate. Wipe thoroughly with a tack cloth. Seal the plate on both sides with a penetrating wood sealer. Allow to dry for thirty minutes. Lightly sand the plate again and wipe with the tack cloth.

Make a mixture of 6 parts DecoArt Americana Titanium White to 1 part Warm Neutral. Thin this mixture with water to a flowing consistency. You do not want the paint so thin that it's transparent, nor do you want it so thick that ridges form in the basecoat.

Basecoat the plate with two coats of this acrylic mixture, allowing the paint to dry completely between coats. When the final coat is dry, sand very lightly with Super Film ultra-fine grain sanding film.

Using gray graphite, transfer the pattern to the plate. Transfer only the most necessary lines. The lines should be fine, but clearly visible. The more accurate your pattern, the easier it will be to paint.

Basic Flesh Mix
Titanium White + a touch of
Red Iron Oxide + a touch of
Naples Yellow + a pin dot of
Dioxazine Purple

Shading Flesh Mix
basic flesh mix + more Red Iron
Oxide + more Naples
Yellow + a pin dot of Burnt
Umber + a pin dot of Dioxazine
Purple

Highlight Flesh Mix
Titanium White + a pin dot of
Naples Yellow

Blush Mix
Naphthol Red Medium + Burnt
Umber + a touch of Dioxazine
Purple + a touch of Naples
Yellow + a touch of Titanium
White

Mauve Mix
blush mix + Titanium White + a
touch of Naples Yellow

Dark Brown Mix
Burnt Umber + Dioxazine
Purple

Black-Green Mix
Phthalo Blue Red Shade + Burnt
Umber + a touch of Naphthol
Red Medium

Painting Procedure

You will paint Santa in gradual layers of transparent and semitransparent glazes, using water as the glazing medium. These glazes are used to build depth, to add accent hues and to build lights and highlights. Predampen the surface with clean water prior to almost every step in the painting. The predampening gives you more time to complete each step before the paint dries. It also helps to ease out any color lines in your application. You will also use water to thin the paint to the proper value, transparency and consistency.

Develop the project in the following manner: Paint a step in one area; while that step is drying, go to another area and paint a step. When the first area is dry, you may return to it to add or repeat steps. This allows you to develop all areas of the project simultaneously and helps avoid overworking. At times, you will be adding several steps to small areas within a larger segment of the composition. Do this only when space permits you to work without disturbing other wet areas.

The order normally used for acrylic projects is:

1. Basecoat area with one or more colors. The instructions may call for a solid wash basecoat or a side-loaded basecoat. More than one application may be needed.

2. Next, shade the area. Shading is normally done with a side-loaded brush. More than one shading color may be called for in the instructions. Shading may be applied as many times as necessary to achieve the desired depth of color.

3. Add tints or accent colors next. There may be more than one tint in any given segment of your composition.

4. Now build the light and highlight values. More than one application is usually needed to achieve the desired level of brightness in the highlights.

5. Add details to each area last. Linework, strokes, dots and secondary subject matter—such as Santa's holly and ribbon—are normally painted in the detail steps.

1 With the ½-inch (12mm) angle brush, thin some basic flesh mix with water to make a medium value wash. Take some time in loading the brush on the palette so that the wash is an even value. With a clean brush, carefully predampen all flesh areas with water, staying within the outer face and hand lines. Dampen slightly into the beard where it grows from the face. Blot the brush loaded with the basic flesh mix and basecoat the face and hand. Do this with a minimum of strokes. Allow these areas to dry. The basecoats will be slightly transparent. If they are too transparent or too pale in value, you may repeat the basecoat steps when the area is thoroughly dry. The pattern lines should still show through the basecoat. In the same manner as you painted the flesh, basecoat all beard, hair and fur areas with a medium-value wash of the highlight flesh mix. You may work these areas as one unit, dampening and basecoating over the pattern lines between areas.

2 Side load the ½-inch (12mm) angle brush with the mauve
mix. Blend the brush carefully on the palette to achieve a
good gradation of color in the side load. Dampen the hat with
clean water, then apply the mauve mix with the paint side of
the brush turned toward the darker areas of the basecoat. (The
clear side of the brush should be toward the light and highlight
areas.) Walk the color out until the desired width of color is
achieved, but don't cover all the light background color in the
highlight areas. Dampen the shoulder and sleeve areas with
clean water, pulling the moisture lower at the bottom than you
wish the color to go. This will allow the color to fade into the
background. Basecoat as you did for the hat, holding the color
side of the brush toward the areas under the fur trim. Walk
the color out until it fades into the damp background.

Dampen the fur areas of the coat and hat with clean water.
Apply a pale wash of Burnt Umber to the fur with a fully
loaded ½-inch (12mm) angle brush. Load the wash as described in step one.

3 Dampen the face with clean water. Side load the ¼-inch (6mm) or ⅜-inch (10mm) angle brush with the shading flesh mix and apply the first shading value to the outer edges of the face. While this is drying, dampen the hand and apply the shading flesh mix to the lower side of the hand, curving up to the wrist along the cuff. Return to the face while this area dries. Add another section of shading to the face; while this is drying, return to the hand and shade again. Continue to alternate between the face and hand until the shading areas are complete.

Change to the smaller ⅛-inch (3mm) angle brush or a small round brush to paint the shaded areas of the nose, the eyelid creases and the wrinkles in the forehead and nose bridge. If you switch to a round brush, dampen the area, apply the color, then soften or blend the edges with the corner of a damp angle brush. Using the same procedure as outlined for the face, apply the first shading color to the hat and coat. Use the ½-inch (12mm) angle brush and a stronger value of the mauve mix.

Now shade the beard and hair. Use the ¼-inch (6mm) or ⅜-inch (10mm) brush, side loaded in the black-green mix. Blend the brush on the palette until you have a soft gray-green value in the brush. Dampen the beard and hair. First apply the soft shadows around the hand, holly and ribbon, under the mouth and nose and around the mustache. Return to a dry area and add the flowing S-curve darks that give direction to the hair and beard. Also add lengthwise darks to the mustache. Next, add the first shading to the fur with stronger values of Burnt Umber. Use the ½-inch (12mm) angle brush on the collar and sleeve. You may wish to change to a ⅜-inch (10mm) or ¼-inch (6mm) angle when shading the hat and tassel. Paint the fur in much the same manner as the beard and hair: Paint the shadow areas first, then add the flowing darks. The fur should be loose and choppy.

4 Begin this step by adding a deeper shading value to the face and hand. Side load a ⅜-inch (10mm) angle brush with the dark brown mix. For smaller areas, you may wish to change to a smaller angle or round brush, as you did in the previous steps. Apply the deeper shading in the same manner as the first shading. This darker value should stay within the first shading, tucking into the deepest recess areas.

Next, add two dark values to the hat and coat. First use the blush mix; when that's dry, strengthen the deepest recesses with the dark brown mix. In the beard and hair, strengthen the dark areas with stronger black-green mix. Brush mix the dark brown mix + the black-green mix in the side load of your brush and apply a darker value to the fur.

5 You're now ready to apply tints to the face. First, side load the ⅜-inch (10mm) angle brush with the blush mix. Dampen the face and apply this color to the lower cheek curve, walking the color up until it softens into the ball of the cheek. Then apply small touches of the blush mix at the blending edges of the four curved shadow areas around each eye, at the edge of the forehead shading and on the lower curve of the ball of the nose. Also apply the blush mix to the curved edge of the shading at the back of the hand and at the edge of the lower, curved finger shadows.

You don't see much of Santa's mouth, just a hint of a lower lip. Paint this by side loading the ⅛-inch (3mm) angle brush with blush mix + shading flesh mix. Stroke across the lip, with the color side of the brush turned toward the lower edge. Allow this to dry, then apply a narrower side load of blush mix + dark brown mix to the same area.

Next, tint the fur with the beard shading color and the beard with the fur shading color. This will help tie these two very different color areas together. Thin some of the black-green mix to a pale gray tint and side load it on a ½-inch (12mm) angle brush. Dampen the fur with clean water and apply the tint to the blending edges of the dark and medium areas, softening out into the light areas. Then apply tints of the dark brown mix to the beard with a side-loaded brush. Add these tints to the blending edges of most shaded areas.

6 To add a soft, gray-green background to your painting, dampen an area much larger than the actual background and apply black-green mix with a side-loaded ¾-inch (19mm) angle brush. Dampening a larger area than needed will make it much easier to fade the background color into the plate color. To achieve soft movement in the background, pull some vertical and some horizontal brushstrokes as you walk the color out. At this time, you may take the soft black-green into any area of the painting that you wish to subdue or push into the background. Areas where this is useful are on both sides of the hat where it curves around Santa's head, on both sides of the collar where it curves around to Santa's back, and in the foreground to subdue the inner cuff area and the lower beard.

Apply highlights to the upper right of the ball of Santa's cheeks with the highlight flesh mix, side loaded in the ¼-inch (6mm) angle brush. Turn the color side of the brush inward and stroke around a small circle. The blending side of the brush will face outward, giving a soft, blended edge to the highlight. Now load the highlight flesh mix into a small round brush. Apply a highlight to the upper right side of the ball of

the nose and on the right side of Santa's forehead, between the wrinkles. Keep a damp brush handy for softening the highlights applied with a round brush. Finally, apply highlights to the upper area of the hand.

Paint Santa's eyebrows with the point of the round or liner brush using tiny strokes of the highlight flesh mix. Allow to dry, then paint dark lines at the base of the brows with the black-green mix. Add a few dark touches of black-green mix along the upper edge of the brows. Allow to dry and, if needed, highlight the brows with strokes of the highlight flesh mix.

Add dark linework within the fur areas and at the outer edges with the dark brown mix and a mixture of the dark brown mix + the black-green mix. When dry, apply light lines with Naples Yellow and a mix of Naples Yellow + the highlight flesh mix. Pull some of these light lines inward, toward the darks. In the same manner, apply linework to the beard and hair. Paint dark lines with the black-green mix or a mixture of the black-green mix + the dark brown mix. Paint the light lines with a mixture of the highlight flesh mix + a small amount of Naples Yellow, or simply use straight highlight flesh mix.

Painting the Eyes

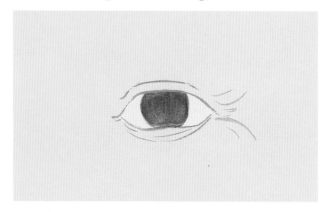

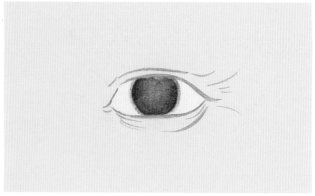

7 Without dampening the ground, use a small round brush to basecoat the white of one of the eyes with highlight flesh mix and the iris area with a strong wash of Burnt Umber. While the first eye is drying, paint the second eye. You should be able to alternate between eyes with each progressive step.

8 Dampen the iris area. Apply a dark line at the outer edge of the iris with the dark brown mix. If needed, soften with the point of your round brush. Next, paint a pale line around the edge of the iris with very thin dark brown mix.

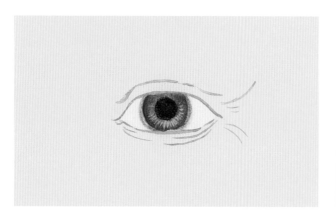

9 Dampen the iris and highlight with tiny round brush-strokes of Naples Yellow. When dry, brighten the lower right quarter of the iris circle by repeating the previous step. Allow this to dry, and paint the pupil with the round brush loaded with black-green mix.

10 Paint the upper lid line and lashes with a round brush loaded with a mixture of the dark brown mix + the black-green mix. Begin the lid line as a fine line at the inner corner of the eye and broaden it as it crosses the center of the eye. As you approach the outer corner, release pressure so that the line thins again. Pull the lashes in both directions, with a change point in the center of the eye. Make the lashes shortest where they are coming straight toward you. Paint the lower lid line with the dark brown mix, making it finer and softer in value than the upper lid line. Don't extend this line out as far on either side as the upper lid line; it should stop just short of the upper lid line. If you wish, use this color to indicate an inner corner on the eye. Pull tiny, soft lashes from the lower lid line toward the outer corners. Apply a shadow of the dark brown mix + the black-green mix to the inner eye. Side load the color into a small angle brush and paint the shadow with the color side of the brush against the upper lid line. Allow to dry, then apply the same color at the inner and outer corners of the eye, curving across the triangle in that area.

Painting the Holly, Pine and Ribbon

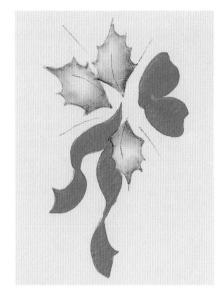

11 Paint the ribbon with a solid basecoat of the mauve mix. Use a brush that's about the same width as the ribbon—a no. 6 flat will probably be about right. You may need to apply a second coat of color. Basecoat the leaves with a ¼-inch (6mm) angle brush side loaded in the black-green mix. Apply the color to the triangle at the base of the leaf and loosely around the edges. Keep the first application relatively soft.

12 Shade the ribbon with the ¼-inch (6mm) angle brush, side loaded with the blush mix. The shading begins to define the loops, the darks where the ribbon disappears into the holly and the various twists and turns of the streamers.

Add a side load of stronger black-green mix to the leaves at the base and along one side. When dry, dampen again and pull soft darks in the vein areas with a round brush and the same color.

13 To give sharper definition to the ribbon, apply deeper shading with the dark brown mix. This value should stay within the previous shading.

With the black-green mix in your liner brush, apply loose, broken lines to the outer leaf edges. Also pull points on the leaves and add sharp vein lines.

Paint the first value in the pine with the point of the round or liner brush loaded in the black-green mix. Give the pine a nice, thick base with these strokes. This illustration shows the background color which you painted previously.

14 Dampen the ribbon and add highlights with a round brush loaded with a mixture of the mauve mix + a touch of highlight flesh mix. Keep a damp brush handy to soften as needed. Build the highlights with at least one more application of this color. Should your highlights become too bright or chalky, simply glaze over them with a pale wash of the blush mix.

Add tiny highlight strokes to the pine with a mixture of the black-green mix + a touch of Naples Yellow + a touch of the highlight flesh mix. Keep the strokes much finer and fewer than the original basecoating strokes. Add dot berries to your holly with a mixture of the dark brown mix + the blush mix; the blush mix; and a mixture of the blush mix + the mauve mix. When the dots are dry, you may highlight some with the mauve, basic flesh and highlight flesh mixes.

Painting the Plate Border

When trimming any project, remember that the trim is secondary. In this case, the Santa is the primary subject matter. He should remain the focal point, with the border as a complementary accent. Because you don't want to overpower the Santa, keep the border simple and subdued.

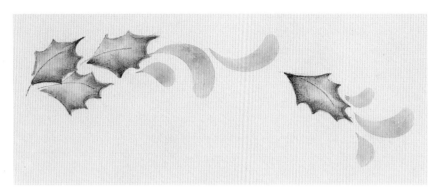

15 Load a no. 8 filbert brush in a pale wash of the mauve mix + the dark brown mix. Blot the brush on a towel and paint all comma strokes in the border design. Paint the holly leaves with the same steps as you did for the inner plate design, using a pale side load of the black-green mix to base them.

16 Dress the comma strokes with small "point-press" strokes, using a liner and a stronger value of the mauve + dark brown brush mixture. To make a point-press, hold the liner brush on its tip, perpendicular to the surface. Pull toward you, keeping the liner brush on its tip, then sit the brush down on its tip to make the head of the stroke. Shade the holly with stronger values of the black-green mix.

17 Create pockets for latticework with additional point-press strokes. Apply these strokes and the latticework with the liner brush and a mixture of the mauve mix + the dark brown mix. Line the holly leaves with the black-green mix.

18 Add dot berries of the mauve mix + the dark brown mix. Add a few accent dots of the black-green mix + a touch of Naples Yellow + a touch of Titanium White. Add a few filler wisps with the green mixture.

Finishing Your Project

Side load a ¾-inch (19mm) angle brush with a mixture of the mauve mix + the dark brown mix and blend on the palette until you achieve a very pale load. Dampen all beaded edges of the plate with a large brush. Place the color side of the side-loaded brush against a beaded edge and pull around the plate. Try not to interrupt the stroke any more than necessary. Repeat this step until you have placed color against every beaded edge. You will need to change to a smaller brush to shade against the bead on the inside of the plate.

When all painting is complete, varnish your piece with a good quality waterbase varnish. Use a large, synthetic brush and apply six to ten coats, allowing each to dry thoroughly and wiping with a tack cloth between coats. When the varnishing is complete, treat the piece with a coat of J.W. etc. Painter's Finishing Wax.

Glorious Angel Sconce

When we moved from Louisiana recently, I left longtime students and friends. Many of them had painted with me since the 1970s, and had become family. I promised them that I would return once or twice a year for what we have titled "homecoming seminars." I designed the "Glorious Angel Sconce" for our first homecoming seminar.

This particular angel could be displayed year-round, or solely during the Christmas season. She is done in nontraditional Christmas colors. I encourage my students to use different color combinations according to their decorating needs or the use of a particular piece. Several students in the seminar painted their angel sconces on a Grey Sky DA111 background and used Deep Midnite Blue DA166 or Midnite Blue DA85 for the darker areas. Several others used Silver Sage Green DA149 or Ice Blue DA135 for the light areas and trimmed the piece in Deep Teal DA116 or Midnite Blue DA85 (all the above colors are by DecoArt Americana). If you're going to display the angel year-round and you do not like the metallic

MATERIALS

Palette

Winsor & Newton Finity Artists' Acrylics
- Burnt Umber
- Dioxazine Purple
- Gold Ochre
- Naphthol Red Medium
- Naples Yellow
- Phthalo Blue Red Shade
- Red Iron Oxide
- Renaissance Gold
- Silver
- Titanium White

DecoArt Americana Acrylic Paints
- Black Plum DA172
- French Mocha DA188
- Light Buttermilk DA164
- Warm Neutral DA90

Surface

The angel sconce is available from Brenda Stewart by Design, 228 Yorkshire Dr., Williamsburg, VA 23185; phone (757) 564-7093.

Winsor & Newton Brushes
- Series 7 no. 0 or no. 1 Kolinsky sable round
- Series 545 ¼-inch (6mm), ½-inch (12mm) and ¾-inch (19mm) square combs
- Series 560 ⅛-inch (3mm), ⅜-inch (10mm), ½-inch (12mm) and ¾-inch (19mm) or 1-inch (25mm) synthetic angles
- Series 740 no. 1 or no. 2 red sable liner
- Series 5977 no. 1 or no. 3 hog bristle fan brush

Medium

Winsor & Newton Acrylic Flow Improver, diluted mix

Other

Small- to medium-sized natural sea sponge with small texture

This pattern may be hand-traced or photo-copied for personal use only. Enlarge at 161 percent to return to full size.

accents, you may delete them.

Another factor you may vary on this project is the way the sconce is turned. Painted as she is now, the angel seems to be looking down at the candle. You may decide to turn the sconce the other way and set something on top of the shelf. This is just as nice, but will give a slightly different effect.

I designed this project to be a bit less time-consuming than some of the others in this book. If you are a teacher, your students need a break from intense, time-consuming projects. If you paint to sell, you need to be able to offer a variety of price points. A painting that has taken less time to paint may, unless painted on a very costly object, be offered for a more moderate price than those taking more time. If you simply paint for your own enjoyment, you need an occasional break from more difficult projects. Paint this one for enjoyment!

Preparation

If you are painting the project on the sconce that is shown, disassemble the piece for preparation. Sand all surfaces and wipe with a tack cloth. Seal the front and back surfaces and the edges of all pieces with a penetrating wood sealer. Allow this to dry for thirty minutes. Lightly sand the pieces again and wipe with the tack cloth.

Make a mixture of 10 parts Light Buttermilk + 2 parts Warm Neutral + 1 part French Mocha. Thin this paint with water to a strong value wash consistency. Basecoat the surface the angel is to be painted on with two coats of this mixture. Allow time for complete drying between coats. When the final coat is dry, sand very lightly with Super Film ultra-fine grain sanding film. Wipe with a tack cloth.

Basecoat all remaining surfaces of the piece, including the edges, with Black Plum, adding just enough water to the paint to obtain a flowing consistency. Two coats should adequately cover the surface. Allow for complete drying between coats.

Transfer the angel pattern with gray graphite paper. Transfer only the most necessary lines. The lines should be fine, but clearly visible. If needed, transfer outer placement lines for the strokework on the sconce brackets, using white graphite. The lines should be barely visible. If possible, do the strokework with no pattern.

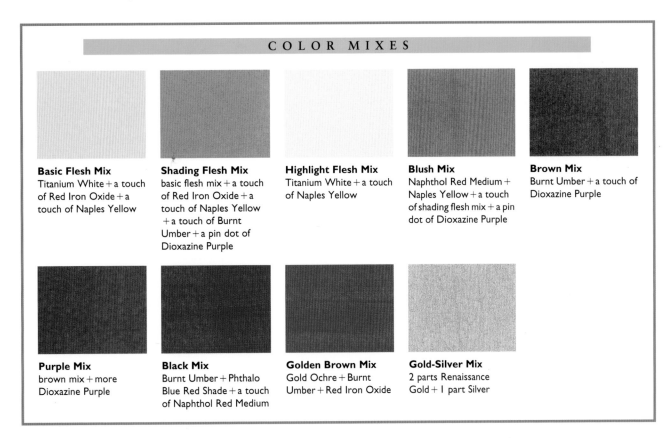

COLOR MIXES

Basic Flesh Mix
Titanium White + a touch of Red Iron Oxide + a touch of Naples Yellow

Shading Flesh Mix
basic flesh mix + a touch of Red Iron Oxide + a touch of Naples Yellow + a touch of Burnt Umber + a pin dot of Dioxazine Purple

Highlight Flesh Mix
Titanium White + a touch of Naples Yellow

Blush Mix
Naphthol Red Medium + Naples Yellow + a touch of shading flesh mix + a pin dot of Dioxazine Purple

Brown Mix
Burnt Umber + a touch of Dioxazine Purple

Purple Mix
brown mix + more Dioxazine Purple

Black Mix
Burnt Umber + Phthalo Blue Red Shade + a touch of Naphthol Red Medium

Golden Brown Mix
Gold Ochre + Burnt Umber + Red Iron Oxide

Gold-Silver Mix
2 parts Renaissance Gold + 1 part Silver

Painting Procedure

When painting the angel sconce, one important thing to consider is the mood of the piece. The entire painting is soft and loose. The face, which is the focal point within the center of interest area, has sharper detail and greater value and contrast. The hair and wings are much softer and more subdued. This is achieved by loosening edges, using less detail and minimizing contrast with the background color; in fact, you will actually pull the background color into or float it over these areas to subdue them.

Begin the painting by basecoating the face, wings and hair. When all areas have been basecoated, return to the first area and adjust the basecoating as needed. Moving from area to area will enable a step to thoroughly dry before you add another. It also enables you to develop all areas of the painting at the same time. This will help you achieve a better balance of values throughout the project.

Add shading values next, then the tints and highlights. Next, add details to the various areas and apply the background. When the background is applied, look for areas that need to be "pulled out" or emphasized by adding more dark around them. Also feed the dark from one area into the shadow points of another. This will relieve the "cut and paste" look of the painting and will make your angel seem to be a part of the "atmosphere" or space that she is resting in. You may also wash the background color over an area to subdue it slightly. I did this along the back edges of the wings.

Complete the painting by adding some detail over the background. An example of this is the linework added at the outer edges of the hair. I develop the primary focal area first, then design and complete the other project surfaces. They must be kept secondary to the focal point area.

Brenda Stewart

Pattern for sconce brackets. This pattern may be hand-traced or photocopied for personal use only. Shown at full size.

Painting the Face, Hair and Wings

These first three illustrations show the first stages in the development of the face, hair and wings. I've demonstrated these elements in the same order that I actually used to develop the project.

1 Using a ½-inch (12mm) angle brush, fully and evenly loaded with paint, basecoat the face area with a medium-strong value of the basic flesh mix. Since this area is rather small, you should be able to accomplish this without dampening the surface first. Paint through all pattern lines—they will show through the wash.

While the face is drying, fully and evenly load a ¾-inch (19mm) angle brush with a pale wash of the highlight flesh mix. Dampen the wings; since this is a large area, dampening the surface prior to applying the paint will give you time to apply a more even basecoat. Paint through all pattern lines on the wings. These lines will show through the basecoat wash. Only a portion of the wings are shown on the example. Paint the lower wing feathers in the same manner as the longer feathers in the section shown.

Next, dampen the hair area, pulling the moisture out beyond the ends of the hair. Load a ½-inch (12mm) angle brush in a pale value of the golden brown mix. Load the brush fully and evenly and apply this color to the hair. As you approach the ends of the hair, lift the brush to its corner to trail these areas out into the background.

Repeat these basecoating steps on each area as many times as needed to obtain the desired value or a more even basecoat.

Returning to the face, apply the first shading value with a side-loaded brush of the shading flesh mix + the basic flesh mix. Dampen the face prior to applying the shading. Use a ½-inch (12mm) angle brush for applying the larger shaded area. Change to a smaller angle brush as

needed.

Place the first of these shadings along the hairline, curving along the lower edge of the chin. Next, apply shading in front of the eye, in the upper eyelid crease, in the crease forming the fatty tissue under the eye and in the brow. Notice that the shading placed in front of the eye curves upward toward the brow and down toward the nose, creating the cheek curve.

Paint shaded areas around the flare of the nostril, inside the nostril and on the underside of the nose, pulling down to the upper lip. Do not attempt to do

all of these in the nose area at one time. Apply one, allow it to dry while working elsewhere, then return to add another to the area. A ⅛-inch (3mm) angle brush is perfect for these smaller areas. Also paint shading, curving from the nose back toward the corner of the mouth. This creates or defines the lower cheek curve. The last shading is a small touch above the ball of the chin, under the lower lip. This rests against the front edge of the face.

While the face is drying, apply the first shading on the wings with a brush side loaded with the brown mix. Use as large a brush as you can comfortably work with in the area to accomplish this step. I suggest using a combination of the ½-inch (12mm) and ¾-inch (19mm) angle brushes. Dampen the wings before adding a step. For the larger, softer shading areas, dampen the surface a bit more than for the darker, more definitive areas. In these darker, more sharply defined areas, barely skim the surface with a damp brush prior to applying the shading. Apply the darker, more defined shadings with a darker side load of the brown mix than you used for the softly shaded areas.

Apply the areas of definitive shading first. A definitive shadow normally has one definite or sharp edge and one softening or blending side. The definitive edge of the shading rests against the object being defined by the darker value. These are sometimes referred to as shadow points, because they are where two objects or portions of objects overlap. In the wings, these are the shaded areas that separate the wings, the sections of the wings or the individual "feathers" of the wings. There is also shading on the wings at the point where they descend behind the head.

Apply the softer wing shadings next. Paint them just off the edge of the outer wing areas. Begin at the head, go over the "shoulder" of the wings and continue along the outer or back edge of the front wing.

Next, shade the hair. Use the brown mix, side loaded in a ⅜-inch (10mm) or ½-inch (12mm) angle brush. Dampen the surface slightly prior to painting. Place a strong, definitive shadow against the outer edge of the angel's face. Paint a somewhat softer and wider shading all along the outer back edge of the head. Next, add a shadow along the part line and a bit at the left, outer crown edge. All other shadow points have to do with the way the hair flows and overlaps. Apply them loosely with the color side of the brush turned sometimes toward the face and sometimes away from it.

2 Next, deepen the shading on the face with a brush side loaded with the shading flesh mix. Use the size of angle brush that is appropriate for the area you are shading. Dampen the face very slightly prior to shading. Keep the darker value in a smaller area within the initial shading.

Now you are ready to add the blush mix to the face. Dampen and apply this color with a side-loaded brush. Apply it to the cheek, the lower tip of the nose and in the blending edges of the shadows at the chin, forehead and temple. Keep this tint relatively soft; I have made it a bit stronger than usual on this angel because of the strong contrast and glowing effect of the face.

Deepen the shaded areas of the wings and hair next. Apply the brown mix + a touch of the black mix, side loaded in an appropriately sized angle brush. Dampen the surface prior to application. Add this in the deepest areas of shadows and keep it within the first shading value as instructed for the face shading. Look for triangular-shaped areas. They should be among the darkest areas within the wings and hair.

3 Side load a ⅜-inch (10mm) angle
brush with a very pale value of the
purple mix. Dampen the face and apply
the purple to the shaded area of the face
as a glazed tint. It should not darken,
but rather change the hue to a cooler
color. Add this same tint to some of the
shaded areas throughout the hair, extending it a bit beyond the shaded area
into the medium values of the hair. Do
not apply it to every dark in the hair.

Next apply highlights to the face
with a ⅜-inch (10mm) angle brush side
loaded in the highlight flesh mix. Apply
these highlights very strongly to create a
glow on the face. Dampen each area just
slightly prior to painting. Apply on the
front edge of the forehead, the tip of the
nose, the front curve of the cheek and
the front curve of the ball of the chin.

Add some wing detail with a liner
and the ¼-inch (6mm) or ½-inch
(12mm) comb brush. First, use a liner
brush to paint very pale lines for the
veins in the predominant feathers. Use a
very thinned mixture of the purple
mix + a touch of the black mix. Next,
load the ¼-inch (6mm) comb brush with
the same dilute mixture. Rake from the
vein outward on the back or right side
of the predominant feathers. Pull the
strokes on a slight downward slant from
the vein. Pull inward with very short
strokes of the comb on the left side of
the predominant feathers. Pull these
strokes in, on an upward slant, toward
the vein.

Now add some detail highlighting to
the feathers with the gold-silver mix.
Apply this with the comb also. Pull the
strongest gold-silver from the front or
outer left edge of the feathers. Pull at an
upward slant, toward the vein. Pull
short strokes of this color at the tips of
the back or right edge of the feathers.

Painting the Eye

4 Next, paint the face details. First, basecoat the white of the eye with the highlight flesh mix loaded in the point of the small round brush. Allow this to dry. With the tip of the round brush, paint a medium value of the brown mix in the iris. Allow this to dry. With the tip of the small round brush, add a pupil with the black mixture.

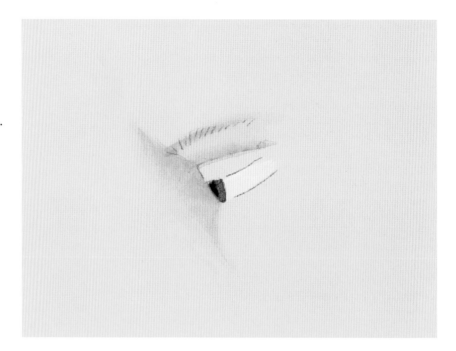

5 Paint the lid lines and lashes with the small round brush and the brown mix + a touch of the black mix. Paint the upper lid line a bit darker and heavier. Pull the lashes at a downward slant from this line, making them shorter as they approach the back corner of the eye. Paint the lower lid line with a bit more of the brown color in the brush mixture, using a finer line. Add the brows with very light, thin lines of the brown mix + a pin dot of the black mix.

Painting the Mouth

6 Basecoat the mouth with a pale value mixture of the shading flesh mix + the blush mix. You may use the tip of a small round brush for basecoating. Next, side load a ⅛-inch (3mm) angle brush with the blush mix + a touch of the purple mix and shade the lower edges of the mouth.

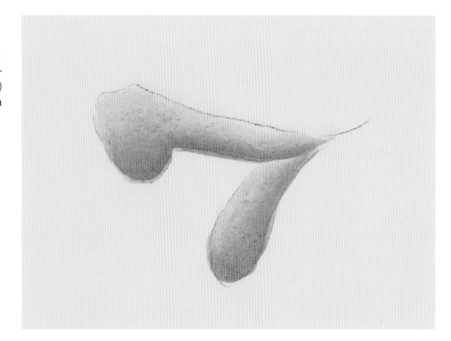

7 Highlight the mouth toward the upper side of each lip with a side load of the highlight flesh mix + a touch of the basic flesh mix. Use a side-loaded ⅛-inch (3mm) angle brush for this step. Finally, add very fine accent lines with the blush mix + a touch of the purple mix.

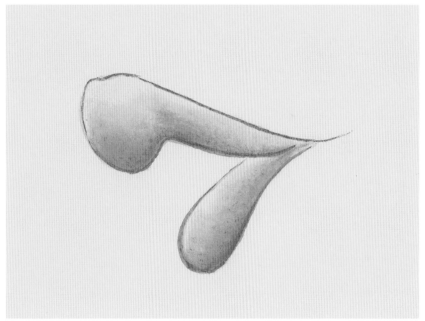

Detailing the Hair and Applying the First Background Color

8 Begin to paint the background color with Black Plum side loaded into a ¾-inch (19mm) angle brush. Dampen the surface to allow maximum working time. Do not try to apply all background areas in one painting. Allow a step to dry, then add more color to expand, smooth or darken the background. More dark is painted in the background on the back or right side of the angel and on the left, under her head. The background is paler and narrower on the left side of the angel. Paint some predominant triangular areas that are darker. Place one under the angel's head where the wing curves around it. Place another in the very open triangle where the back wing disappears behind the head. Paint a third area where the two wings overlap and then part, forming an open triangle in the background. The finished project on page 51 shows that there are also very small triangles where the feathers part at the end of the wings. Paint these triangular openings in the background somewhat darker. At any point where a dark area of the hair or wings opens into the background, pull some of this color to push the angel into the space she is resting on. Also apply it in a wide, soft float at the back side of the wing to subdue that area, and add it softly as a tint color throughout the wings.

Add dark and light linework into the hair with the liner brush. Use the brown mix or a mixture of the brown mix + a touch of the black mix for the dark and Naples Yellow for the light.

Keep the lighter linework mostly on the left side of the head and on the front half of the right side of the head. All linework should accent the flow of the hair and also loosen the feeling of the hair—notice that it tends to fly away at the outer edges and the ends.

Add a fine combing of the gold-silver mix to the hair with a ¼-inch (6mm) comb brush. Apply the color more heavily on the left side of the face and on the forward portion of the right side of the hair.

When you are working with metallics, always turn the piece at different angles in the light to check the amount of metallic accent. It may appear that you have no metallic on the piece at all from one angle, but from a different angle, the gold-silver may scream at you.

Highlight the front edges of the wings with a very soft side load of the gold-silver mix, loaded in a ½-inch (12mm) or ¾-inch (19mm) angle brush. You may also stroke a touch of this side load into the more undefined feather layers toward the upper portion of the wings.

Finishing the Background

This illustration shows the background, complete with sponging and wind swirls. I've shown these without the painted angel so that you may more clearly see where they are applied.

9 Dampen a small-textured sea sponge. Load one edge in Black Plum. Soften the load in the sponge by tapping it on the wet palette. Dampen the entire background area with a ¾-inch (19mm) or 1-inch (25mm) angle brush. Beginning in the deeper value background areas, tap in the Black Plum sponging. Each time you pick the sponge up from the surface, turn it a different way before setting it back down. Carry the sponge-work from the darker areas out into the lighter areas of the background. When you reach the paler areas on the left, the sponge should have less paint in it, and will give a softer sponging value. If any area of the sponging is too harsh, simply soften it by tapping over it with the unloaded back side of the sponge.

After the sponging is dry, side load Black Plum into a ¾-inch (19mm) or 1-inch (25mm) angle brush and float it all around the perimeters of the angel surface (see page 51).

The last step on this portion of the painting is to apply the wind swirls. Paint these with a ¾-inch (19mm) comb brush, loaded in Black Plum. Pull them from the right edge of the surface, curving across toward the left. Do not pull the swirls all the way across the surface. Keep them shorter in the area of the angel's head. Pull them in a gentle S-curve. When the Black Plum swirls are dry, repeat this step, using the gold-silver mix.

Painting the Sconce Brackets

10 First, paint a relatively wide side load of the gold-silver mix in the strokework. Apply the paint with a ½-inch (12mm) angle brush, with the color side of the brush turned toward the back or outer curve of the stroke.

11 With a no. 1 or no. 2 liner brush, apply overstrokes and accents of the gold-silver mix. First, pull long, flowing, "dressing" strokes around the comma shapes. As you end these strokes, hesitate a bit at the inside curve of the head of the comma. This creates a soft dot at the end of the stroke.

The remaining strokes are point-press. To make a nice point press, keep the brush perpendicular to the surface. Pull toward you and then sit the brush down on the tip to make the head of the stroke.

The last element you need to add to the strokework is the graduated oval dots. Load the liner with a heavier and somewhat thicker mixture of the gold-silver paint than you used for the strokes. Lay the side of the brush tip down to make the oval dots. Start with the largest one in each group. Progressively graduate to smaller sizes by putting less pressure on the brush as you touch it to the surface.

When the strokework is completely dry, spatter all surfaces basecoated in Black Plum with the gold-silver mix. To spatter, load a small fan brush in slightly thinned paint, then pull a palette knife gently from side to side across the fan bristles. You may wish to test the paint thickness and the heaviness of the load on a practice surface prior to actually spattering the piece.

Finishing Your Project

When you've finished painting the angel and the brackets, spatter all dark basecoated areas with the gold-silver mix. Also apply this mixture to the edges of the piece, over the Black Plum basecoat. I used two coats of the metallic mixture, stroking across the edges. The Black Plum undercoat still shows through and influences the overall appearance of these edges.

When the above steps are complete, allow them to dry thoroughly. Wipe the sections of the unassembled piece with a tack cloth and then apply a good quality waterbase varnish. Use a large synthetic brush and apply six to ten coats. Allow to dry thoroughly and wipe with a tack cloth between coats. When you have completed the varnishing, wax the piece with a coat of J.W. etc. Painter's Finishing Wax and reassemble the sconce.

Victorian Rose Tray

Antique china is one of my collecting passions. The beautiful patterns, detail and colors never fail to inspire me. Much of what I collect has roses as a major portion of the design. This lovely china dresser tray seemed to call for a painting reminiscent of the past.

The roses on the tray are what I term as "trim roses." They are very similar in form and technique to larger roses, except fewer color combinations are used in the undercoating steps and fewer layers are painted in the petal stage. On page 20, you will find a section on basic alkyd techniques. Read this carefully before beginning to paint this project.

This rose design would also be lovely painted on a box basecoated in a pale off-white or gray. Portions of the design could be used on smaller porcelain boxes or bottles. Many blank pieces are available that would enable you to paint a matching vanity set. Let your creativity soar as you contemplate ways to decorate a bedroom or ladies' dressing area around the tray.

MATERIALS

Palette

Winsor & Newton Griffin Alkyds
- Alizarin Crimson
- Burnt Umber
- Cadmium Yellow Light
- Naples Yellow Hue
- Phthalo Blue
- Titanium White

Winsor & Newton Artists' Oil
- Renaissance Gold

Surface

This 9″ × 11″ (23cm × 28cm) china tray is available from Brenda Stewart by Design, 228 Yorkshire Dr., Williamsburg, VA 23185; phone (757) 564-7093.

Winsor & Newton Brushes
- Series 7 no. 0 Kolinsky sable detail round
- Series 240 no. 1 mop
- Series 700 no. 2 sable flat
- Series 760 ⅛-inch (3mm), ¼-inch (6mm), ⅜-inch (10mm) and ½-inch (12mm) sable angles

Loew-Cornell Brushes
- Detail mop
- Mini mop

Medium

Winsor & Newton Blending & Glazing Medium

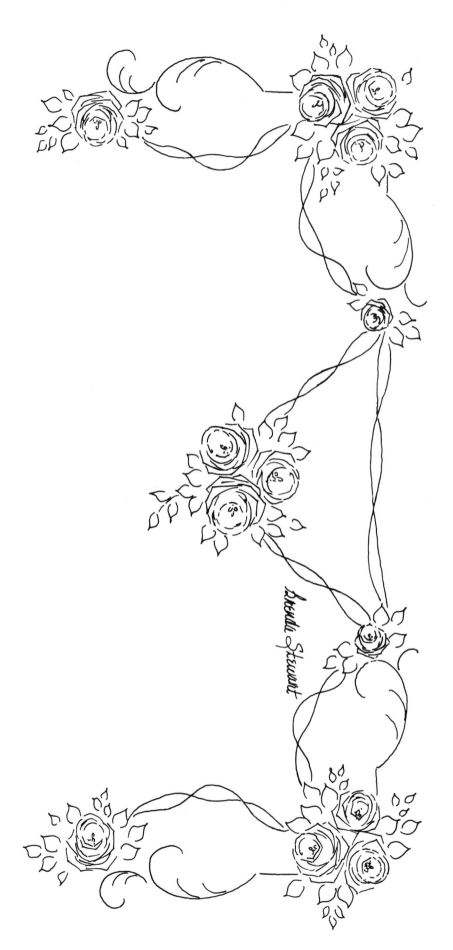

One-half of pattern is shown here. Reverse
tracing for opposite side of tray. This pattern
may be hand-traced or photocopied for
personal use only. Shown at full size.

Preparation

Begin by washing the tray in dishwashing liquid and warm water to remove any dust or oils on the surface. Dry the piece thoroughly. Using gray graphite paper, transfer the pattern to the tray. Transfer only the most necessary lines: If possible, transfer only a circle for rose placements and a fine line for scroll placements. If you can freehand the leaves and ribbon, do so. The fewer lines applied, the better. The lines should be fine, but clearly visible. The pattern given here is one-half of the tray design. Flip the pattern over for the other side of the tray.

The next step is to apply the background color on the tray. Apply a thin coat of Winsor & Newton Blending & Glazing Medium between the outer design lines and the tray edge. With a dry ½-inch (12mm) angle brush, apply a light coat of the light gray mix. Mop this with the no. 1 mop brush until very soft, wiping the brush frequently to remove excess paint.

Using a piece of lint-free cloth or paper towel, gently wipe the perimeter of the tray to remove paint from the embossed design. Mop again to soften any uneven areas left after wiping. Allow the tray to dry overnight, then spray lightly several times with Deco-Art matte acrylic spray before painting the design.

Painting Procedure

The rose tray is developed with a basic painting stage and a second overpainting. In the second stage, you will strengthen, as needed, any steps done in the basic stage and add some steps that are more easily achieved when the first stage is dry. You may divide the work into more stages if you desire.

Prior to painting, apply a scant amount of Winsor & Newton Blending & Glazing Medium to each area. This will enable you to apply small amounts of paint with a dry brush without the surface grabbing the paint. Too much medium will make the surface slippery. If you begin to apply paint and find it will not hold, simply blot the surface with a lint-free tissue or paper towel. Also apply the Blending & Glazing Medium prior to the second stage of painting steps. It's important to keep the paint application light; the goal is a delicate, soft painting. Heavy, thick paint would be out of character for this surface and design, and could cause the small design elements to lack definition or appear muddy.

Finish the first stage of painting in the following order:

1. Undercoat the rose forms with varied color combinations.
2. Set in background colors around the roses.
3. Define the petal edges of the rose with light values.
4. Paint the leaves and shadow leaves around the roses.
5. Paint the ribbon.

After you've completed the first stage, allow the painting to dry. Spray it with several light coats of DecoArt matte acrylic spray, then proceed with the second-stage painting steps:

6. Add color accents or tints to any of the areas painted in the first stage. These tints may be called for in the instructions, or you may apply them as you feel necessary to unify the elements in your painting and to help achieve spatial relationships.
7. Enhance or strengthen any step done in the previous stage. This includes adding brighter highlights or deeper shading.
8. Add filler fern, stems, "wispies" and rose centers.
9. Paint the gold scrollwork.
10. Apply touches of gold to the tray edges.

Dark color mixtures have been thinned slightly so you can see the hue of the color.

Cool Dark Red Mix
Alizarin Crimson + Burnt Umber + a touch of Phthalo Blue

Mauve Mix
cool dark red mix + Titanium White + a touch of Naples Yellow Hue

Warm Dark Red Mix
Alizarin Crimson + a touch of Burnt Umber + a pin dot of Phthalo Blue

Warm Pink Mix
warm dark red mix + Titanium White + Naples Yellow Hue

Brown-Red Mix
Alizarin Crimson + Burnt Umber

Dusty Pink Mix
brown-red mix + Titanium White + Naples Yellow Hue

Black-Green Mix
Burnt Umber + Phthalo Blue

Medium Green Mix
black-green mix + a touch of Cadmium Yellow Light + a touch of Naples Yellow Hue

Yellow-Green Mix
Cadmium Yellow Light + Naples Yellow Hue + a touch of the black-green mix + a pin dot of the brown-red mix + a touch of Titanium White

Gray-Green Mix
Naples Yellow Hue + a touch of the black-green mix + a pin dot of Burnt Umber + a pin dot of Alizarin Crimson + a touch of Titanium White

Light Gray Mix
gray-green mix + a touch of Burnt Umber + a pin dot of Alizarin Crimson + Titanium White

Cream Mix
Titanium White + a touch of Naples Yellow Hue

Painting a Trim Rose

These illustrations will take you through the basic steps of painting a trim rose. Practice on paper until you are comfortable with the construction of the rose.

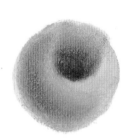

1 With a ¼-inch (6mm) angle brush (use the ⅛-inch [3mm] angle brush for the smallest roses), undercoat the rose with a light application of the mauve, warm pink or dusty pink mix. The mauve mix is the coolest hue, so use more of this mixture on the roses that are under or behind other roses. Use the warm pink or dusty pink mixes on the roses that you want to come forward. You can create an infinite variety of roses by brush mixing between these mixtures.

Next, apply a lighter value to the upper right of the rose and under the imaginary bowl. Use the angle brush side loaded in one of the following mixtures. Use the cream mix + a touch of Naples Yellow Hue on the warmer hued roses. On the cooler roses you may use the cream mix straight, or a brush mixture of the cream mix + a touch of the light gray mix. Wipe your brush and loosely blend the light and medium areas together. Now add a darker crescent to the left and lower curve of the rose. Also apply some of the dark in the center of the rose bowl. Use a side-loaded brush and either the cool dark red mix, the warm dark red mix or the brown-red mix. You may also brush mix various combinations of these colors. Use the dark mixtures that were the root mixture for your rose basecoat. Wipe the brush and blend the darks very lightly into the rose basecoat.

2 Set in background color around the rose with a larger angle brush. Side load the brush with a mixture of the gray-green mix + a touch of black-green mix + a touch of Burnt Umber. Wipe the brush and apply a bit of softer gray-green mix at the outer edges of the background color. Overlap this color into the first background color you applied. With a mini mop, soften the two colors together slightly. Wipe the mop and fade the edges of the background color into the surface background.

Slightly thin the consistency of small puddles of the cream mix, Naples Yellow Hue and the light gray mix with a drop or two of odorless turpentine or paint thinner.

Side load the ¼-inch (6mm) or ⅛-inch (3mm) angle brush with the cream mix + a pin dot of Naples Yellow Hue. For the very cool roses, you may use straight cream mix, or the cream mix + a touch of the light gray mix. The side load should be in a very small area of the brush, toward the tip, and should not be blended as most side loads are. Allow a little light edge to show on the strokes for these steps. With the paint side of the brush turned outward, paint soft, curved petals across the upper back of the rose, using short, broken strokes. Some may overlap the previously painted stroke. Paint two or three layers, coming in toward the center. Pull the ends of these layers slightly downward at the sides. You may wipe and reload the brush as needed.

3 Wipe the brush and side load in thinned cream mix, or the cream mix + a touch of Naples Yellow Hue. (The cream + light gray mix shouldn't be used for this step.) With the color side of the brush turned upward, apply two layers of strokes to the front of the bowl. Try to make these layers appear to connect to the petals that were pulled from the top of the bowl in the previous step. As in the previous step, break these bowl strokes, rather than making them one continuous stroke. Wipe and reload the brush as needed.

4 Wipe the brush and side load once again with the thinned cream mix. Reach up on either side of the rose and pull two strokes that begin to wrap around the front of the rose. When you reach the front of the rose, the brush will be pulling more on the chisel edge. The two strokes shouldn't meet; the end of one stroke should appear to slide under the other. Breaking and restarting these strokes, rather than making them one continuous stroke, will give the petal edges interesting tears and shapes. Wipe and reload the brush as needed.

5 Wipe the brush and side load again in the cream mix. (For cooler roses, use the cream mix + a touch of the light gray mix.) The side load should not be quite as heavy this time, and should be a bit more blended in the brush than for the previous steps. Again pulling from first one side and then the other, pull strokes that seem to come from the sides of the rose and wrap to the front. Hesitate and break the strokes as done in the previous steps. These two strokes may fill the front of the rose; occasionally, a third will be needed in the center to fill an awkward gap.

6 Now you will paint the leaves around the rose. Use a ¼-inch (6mm) or ⅛-inch (3mm) angle brush side loaded in one of the following mixtures: the medium green mix; the medium green mix + a touch of the black-green mix + a touch of Burnt Umber; the yellow-green mix (for the warmest leaves); or the gray-green mix (for the cooler, shadowy leaves). Many leaf colors may be achieved by using various brush mixtures of these colors.

Set the brush at the tip of the leaf, with the color side of the brush outward. Make a short chisel stroke at the tip, and then pull several short overlapping strokes down one side to form the leaf edge. Return to the tip and pull short, overlapping strokes down the other side. Wipe the brush and soften the inside portion of the leaf into the background color. These are meant to be mere suggestions of leaves–they are soft and the back side of the leaf is undefined. The tiny shadow leaves are done in the same manner with the gray-green mix.

Wipe the brush and load it in a light side load of the brown-red mix. Return to any of the darker green leaves, or those done with the medium green or yellow-green mixes, and add red tints to the leaf edges. Apply the color in the same manner as the leaf basecoating, adding as much or as little as you like. You need not add the red tint to every leaf.

Wipe the brush and load it in a light side load of the cool dark red mix. Apply red tints to the cooler shadow leaves and tiny shadow leaves with this mixture, as instructed in the previous steps.

Add the filler fern next. Use the point of your small detail round brush and a mixture of the gray-green + the light gray mixes. Thin the mixture slightly with odorless turpentine or paint thinner. Load the brush in the slightly thinned paint, wipe it and pull wispy stem strokes. Next, paint tiny suggestions of fern leaves on some of the wispy stems by laying the brush on the side of its point and making tiny wiping strokes down each side of the stem.

This illustration also shows the final rose steps, done in the second stage of

the painting. The first stage must be completely dry before completing these steps. Apply a tiny amount of the glazing medium to the area. You may deepen shading colors as needed with a brush side loaded with the original shading color used in the rose + a slightly darker or cooler value. For example, if the dark value in the rose undercoating was the cool dark red mix, you might deepen the area with a mixture of the cool dark red mix + a touch of the black-green mix. If the dark color in the original undercoat was the warm dark red mix, you would use a mixture of the warm dark red mix + a touch of the cool dark red mix, or perhaps straight cool dark red mix. If the dark value in the undercoating stage was the brown-red mix, you might use the cool dark red mix, or the brown-red mix + a touch of the black-green mix. If you are adding a deeper shading color to a very cool shadowy rose, try the cool dark red mix + a touch of the gray-green mix.

You may also add tints or color accents in this stage. It is unlikely that you will need to do much color tinting to

these very small roses. The tints would be added only if the rose color was unacceptable. For instance, if the color were too dull, too brown or too bright, you could tint in correcting hues.

Brighten rose petal edges as needed. Use the small angle brush, side loaded with very small amounts of the original highlight color. Be careful not to overdo this. You don't want to brighten every petal to the same light value, and you *do* want to keep these tiny roses soft and subtle.

Apply the rose centers last. Use the point of your round detail brush, loaded in slightly thinned colors. You will apply small overlapping dots of a dark color first. Use the cool dark red mix + a touch of the black-green mix. Rinse the brush and load with the yellow-green mix + a touch of the brown-red mix + a touch of the cream mix. Apply fewer and smaller light dots on top of the dark ones. Allow these to set up (begin to dry) for a short time, then soften very slightly by patting gently with a small mop brush.

Painting a Ribbon

7 Basecoat the ribbon with the light gray mix and the no. 2 flat brush. Thin the paint with turpentine or paint thinner, just enough so that it will flow easily from the brush. The twisted look of the ribbon is achieved by alternating the brush between chisel and flat positions while pulling along the ribbon length.

8 Next, use the round detail brush and a mixture of the gray-green mix + a touch of the black-green mix + a touch of the cool dark red mix to shade the ribbon. Thin the paint just enough to allow it to flow from the brush when you apply pressure. Pull shading strokes on each ribbon section. Pull from the shaded areas where the ribbon twists or is underneath an object toward the center of each section, lifting the brush from the surface as you approach the center. This will allow the shading strokes to thin and fade away as they enter the lighter areas. Allow the shading to set up for a short period. Soften the shaded areas slightly by pulling over them with a small mop brush.

9 Rinse the dark color out of the round detail brush and load it with slightly thinned cream mix. Starting in the center of each ribbon section, pull highlight strokes toward the darker areas. Lift the brush as you pull toward the darker area so that the strokes thin and fade into the undercoat color. Pull from the center, first in one direction and then in the opposite direction. This will build the highlights brighter in the center of the sections and enable you to fade both ends of the highlights. Allow the highlights to set up for a brief time. Soften the highlight areas slightly by pulling over them with a small mop brush.

Painting Strokework

This illustration shows a section of the gold strokework design. On the left I've shown it broken down into sections to help you understand how to paint the strokework. The right example shows everything connected, as you should paint it. The strokes are done with the round detail brush loaded in Renaissance Gold oil. Thin the paint slightly with turpentine or paint thinner. The paint should flow from the brush, but shouldn't be as thin as for fine linework.

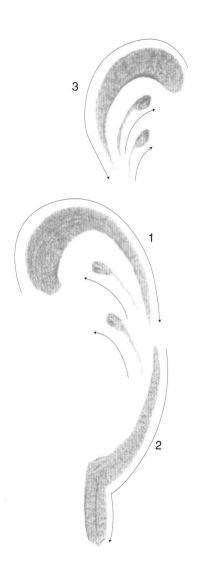

10 Begin with the comma end of the large scroll element. Apply the most pressure to the brush at the head of the comma. Pull in a tight curve, releasing pressure on the brush and thinning out to the tail of the comma. Pull the tail of the comma a bit longer and gradually increase the pressure on the brush again so that the stroke widens back out. Continue to the lower portion of the scroll and then to the straight section. (Don't break the stroke as in the left example; paint the element as one continuous stroke, as shown on the right.)

Add a smaller comma on the back of the first comma, reversing the curve of the larger comma. This is where the scroll design on the long and short sides of the tray are a bit different. On the short side of the tray, the smaller comma is a bit larger than on the long side. It also has the addition of two point-press strokes resting inside it.

The point-press strokes should be added last. Begin with the round detail brush on its point. Pull toward you with a gentle curve. Sit the brush down on the end of the stroke, creating the head. Pull these strokes from the inside of the larger comma strokes.

Painting the Design

The next four illustrations show how a section of the pattern is developed. For detailed instruction on painting the individual elements, refer to the previous illustrations.

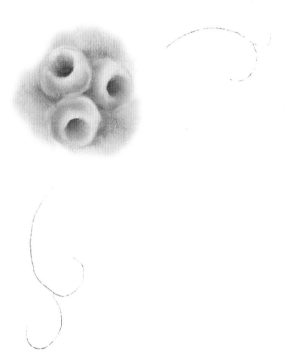

11 Paint the roses through the basecoating steps, blending the colors slightly. Make each rose a slightly different color and use cooler colors in shadow points where one rose is behind another to make some roses recede more.

12 Add a darker shading value to the roses in the crescents, shadow points and centers. Blend this slightly. The addition of background color is also shown in this step. Apply the background colors with a larger angle brush and soften them together with a mop. Fade the edges into the surface background. Notice that the deeper background color is in the triangles formed by the negative spaces between the roses.

13 This illustration shows the petal highlighting and the first leaf placements. Notice that the petals are painted in varying degrees of brightness. The back of the roses are more indistinct, as are some of the lower skirt petals. Apply more predominant highlights to the petals in the more important portions of the roses. The main rose should have the most predominant highlights.

Also notice that the predominant leaves are placed in or near the triangular areas between roses. The exact placement should vary between each rose section. Do not make each design repeat exactly the same. We'll add leaves in the following step to soften the design lines.

14 Place these smaller shadow leaves to further soften the line of the design. They should originate in small triangles between design elements. Your eye will be drawn to gaping triangles in any design. You will instinctively try to fill and soften these angles as your design develops.

The filler fern and rose centers are also shown in this step. Once again, pull the filler fern from small gaps in the design to help fill and soften.

The final addition to this illustration is the gold stroke-work. It and the ribbon sections are the connecting elements between the clusters of roses. Also add small, curved, graduated dot filler here and there throughout the design. It is necessary to give a balanced repetition of gold within the design. Adding the gold work is the last step to complete the design.

Finishing Your Project

When the painting is complete and thoroughly dry, spray the tray with several light coats of DecoArt matte acrylic spray. Wrap a piece of lint-free paper towel or cloth around your index finger. Pick up a small amount of Renaissance Gold oil on the towel and rub on your palette to soften. Wipe the gold across the embossed design areas on the tray edges. Soften as needed by wiping with a clean piece of towel.

When the gold edges are thoroughly dry, apply ten to twelve coats of a spray varnish. I finished this tray with Blair Satin Tole; if you prefer, Blair makes a nice matte finish as well. Before applying, shake the can vigorously for about one minute. Test spray onto a piece of practice paper to be certain the can is spraying evenly. Hold the can as upright as possible, sixteen to eighteen inches from the tray surface. Apply the spray in light coats. Do not spray in extremely humid conditions, in the early morning or at night.

Victorian Rose Tray   65

Vintage Violets

Building and decorating a new home has been an inspiration for my painting. I have chosen a wallpaper for one of the bedrooms that has a violet theme and am developing a number of pieces to coordinate with the wallpaper. Violets are such sweet, dainty flowers, evoking a serene and peaceful feeling. I hope this room will be a place where my grandchildren will want to curl up with a good book, and one that will be a comfortable and cozy guest retreat.

"Vintage Violets" is a soft, low intensity painting, done in white and violet hues with touches of dusty rose. The color mixtures for the project begin to establish color harmony, as they are mixed with root colors that appear over and over throughout the mixtures. The manner in which these hues are used within the painting also helps create color harmony:

- The white violets are shaded with one of the greens plus some of the darker violet.
- Touches of the softer violet tones are also added as color accents and streaks to the white violets.
- The leaves are very muted and grayed and are also accented with colors from the violets.
- The background is predominantly dusty rose, but is shaded here and there with the gray-green and violet.

The overall result is quiet, serene and harmonious. One goal I have in authoring this book is to encourage you, the painter, to see other possibilities for a particular design. Your creativity will develop as you learn to adapt designs for pieces other than the original project surface. This pattern could be broken down into smaller components; for example, the center cluster of white violets would be very appropriate for small porcelain or wood boxes. You could also use this design on journals, guest books, stationery boxes, a small dresser tray, a lotion or soap pump bottle—the possibilities are endless. I am sure you will think of many that I have not suggested.

MATERIALS

Palette
Winsor & Newton Griffin Alkyds
- Alizarin Crimson
- Burnt Umber
- Cadmium Yellow Light
- Naples Yellow Hue
- Phthalo Blue
- Titanium White

Surface
This china mail holder is available from Brenda Stewart by Design, 228 Yorkshire Dr., Williamsburg, VA 23185; phone (757) 564-7093.

Winsor & Newton Brushes
- Series 7 no. 0 or no. 1 Kolinsky sable detail round
- Series 240 no. 1 mop
- Series 700 no. 0 and no. 2 sable flats
- Series 760 ⅛-inch (3mm), ¼-inch (6mm), ⅜-inch (10mm), ½-inch (12mm) sable angles

Loew-Cornell Brushes
- Detail mop
- Mini mop

Medium
Winsor & Newton Blending & Glazing Medium

Front Design

Back Design

These patterns may be hand-traced or photocopied for personal use only.
Shown at full size.

Preparation

Wash the china piece in mild dishwashing liquid and warm water to remove any dust or oils that may be on the surface. Dry the piece thoroughly.

Using gray graphite paper, transfer the most necessary pattern lines to the piece. Don't apply stems, filler ferns or tendrils. The lines should be fine but clearly visible.

Next, apply a thin coat of Winsor & Newton Blending & Glazing Medium to the entire surface, working around pattern lines. Side load a ⅜-inch (10mm) or ½-inch (12mm) angle brush with the dusty rose mix. Apply this to the upper portion of the mail holder, above the design line. Work from the violets and leaves outward, using small, short, uneven

---

COLOR MIXES

Dark color mixtures have been thinned slightly so that you can see the hue of the color.

Dark Red Mix
Alizarin Crimson + Burnt Umber + a pin dot of Phthalo Blue

Dusty Rose Mix
dark red mix + Naples Yellow Hue + a touch of Titanium White

Dark Violet Mix
Phthalo Blue + Alizarin Crimson + a touch of Burnt Umber

Violet Mix
dark violet mix + a touch of Naples Yellow Hue

Red-Violet Mix
violet mix + Alizarin Crimson + Naples Yellow Hue + Titanium White

Gray Mix
violet mix + Burnt Umber + Titanium White

Black-Green Mix
Phthalo Blue + Burnt Umber + a touch of dark violet mix

Medium Green Mix
black-green mix + Naples Yellow Hue + a touch of Cadmium Yellow Light + a pin dot of dark violet mix

Gray-Green Mix
Naples Yellow Hue + a touch of black-green mix + a touch of Titanium White + a pin dot of violet mix

Warm Green Mix
Cadmium Yellow Light + a pin dot of black-green mix + a pin dot of violet mix + Naples Yellow Hue + a touch of Titanium White

Cream Mix
Titanium White + a pin dot of Naples Yellow Hue + a pin dot of dusty rose mix

strokes. After completing the upper area, stroke soft color unevenly along the remaining edges of the piece. Mop this area until the color is very soft. Wipe the mop brush frequently to remove excess paint and medium. On the lower portion of the piece, soften the color until it fades into the porcelain surface. Allow this to dry overnight. Before painting the design, spray lightly several times with DecoArt matte acrylic spray.

Painting Procedure

You will paint the violets in two stages: a first, basic painting stage and a second overpainting. In the second stage, you will strengthen, as needed, any steps done in the basic stage and add some steps that are more easily achieved when the first stage is dry. You may divide the work into more stages if you desire.

Prior to painting, apply a scant amount of Winsor & Newton Blending & Glazing Medium to each area. This will enable you to apply small amounts of paint with a dry brush without the surface grabbing the paint. Too much medium will make the surface slippery. If you begin to apply paint and find it will not

hold, simply blot the surface with a lint-free tissue or paper towel. Also apply the Blending & Glazing Medium prior to the second stage of painting steps. It's important to keep the paint application light; the goal is a delicate, soft painting. Heavy, thick paint would be out of character for this surface and design, and could cause the small design elements to lack definition or appear muddy.

The first stage of the painting is done in the following order:

1. Paint the leaves.
2. Paint the white violets.
3. Paint the purple violets.

After the first stage is completed, allow the painting to dry, then spray it with several light coats of DecoArt matte acrylic spray. When this is dry, proceed with the second stage:

4. Strengthen, as needed, any of the hues or values that were applied to the leaves or flowers in the first painting stage. Highlights on the leaves almost always have to be brightened.
5. Paint the flower centers.
6. Add the green touches to the background.
7. Add stems, flower calyx, tendrils and filler ferns.

Painting the Leaves and White Violets

hese first six illustrations show the steps in painting the leaves and white violets. I've also shown an enlarged violet center in the last illustration to help you interpret the design and understand the construction of a violet. The blossoms are comprised of five petals: a pair of petals at the back or upper portion of the flower, a side pair (one on either side of the blossom) and a front, lead petal.

1 Apply a scant amount of glazing medium to the leaves and the white violets. Side load the ¼-inch (6mm) angle brush with the medium green mix. Apply this color to the darker areas of the first leaf. Wipe the brush. Side load the brush again, this time in the warm green mix + a touch of the cream mix. Apply this color to the lighter areas of the leaf, overlapping the edges of the previously applied color. Wipe the brush, then blend the edges of the two colors together slightly.

Basecoat the second leaf in the same manner, but apply the medium green mix more lightly to this leaf and add more of the cream mix to the warm green + cream brush mixture for the light area. Blend the edges of the colors together slightly, as you did in the first leaf.

The third leaf is an even more muted, shadowy leaf. Basecoat this leaf with the gray-green mix in the darker areas and a very pale mixture of the warm green mix + the cream mix in the lighter areas. Apply the colors and blend the edges together slightly as you did for the first leaf.

Using the no. 2 flat brush, basecoat the white violet petals with the cream mix. Apply an even load of color, with no ridges, to the petals.

Using the round detail brush, shade the violet with the gray mix plus a pin dot of the dark violet mix. You may tip the very end of the brush point in turpentine if the paint won't flow from it, but don't overthin the color. Apply the shading to shadow points (where one area is behind another area). Also pull the color outward from the center of all petals–with the exception of the lead petal—in a manner that will establish the curve of the petals. Using the ⅛-inch (3mm) or ¼-inch (6mm) angle brush, soften the blending edges of the shaded areas into the petal basecoat.

2 Next you will shade the leaves. On the first leaf, side load the ¼-inch (6mm) angle brush with the black-green mix. Apply this to the shadow points, and touch a bit of it along the center vein area. Wipe the brush and blend the edges of this color into the basecoat.

Shade the second leaf in the same manner, but use a stronger value of the medium green mix. Shade the third shadow leaf with a stronger value of the gray-green mix or the gray-green mix + a pin dot of the dark violet mix. After applying each color, wipe the brush and blend the color edges into the basecoat color.

Apply soft red tints to the leaves with a side-loaded brush. Tint the first and second leaves with a very scant brush load of the dark red mix. Tint the third leaf with the violet mix + the red-violet mix. Be very careful to keep them soft. After applying, wipe the brush and blend the tints into the leaf.

Next, apply soft color accents (or tints) to the violets. Use a brush mixture of the violet mix and the red-violet mix. Apply this color with the point of your round detail brush or with a tiny flat brush. Blend the color in very slightly by pulling over it with a mop brush.

3 Using the ⅛-inch (3mm) angle brush side loaded in the
cream mix + the warm green mix, begin to build the highlights in the leaves. Use more of the cream mix and less warm
green mix to highlight the shadow leaf. Build the highlights in
segmented areas on either side of the central vein. Wipe the
brush and blend softly, or you may blend with a mop.

To apply the highlights to the violet petals, load the round
detail brush in the cream mix. Wipe the point of the brush in
turpentine to thin the paint ever so slightly. Stroke the highlights in the high point of each petal. (This will be the point
of the petal that seems to be rolling out toward you the most.)
Lift the brush off of the surface as you pull away from the
high area. You may need to apply this more than once. You
may also strengthen the highlights in the second painting stage.
Using the detail mop, wipe gently over the highlights to soften
them into the petal.

4 Apply the dark violet streaks to the lead petal of the violet with the round detail brush and a brush mixture of the dark violet mix + the dark red mix. You will need to thin the paint by tipping the point of the brush in turpentine and mixing it with the paint. When you touch the point of the brush to the surface and pull, the paint should flow easily from the brush. Using pressure to make the paint flow from the brush will cause the streaks to be too heavy. Allow the streaks to set up for a few minutes, then pull gently over them with the detail mop.

Pull veins in the leaves with the round detail brush. Use the medium green mix + a touch of the black-green mix in the first leaf. Use the medium green mix in the second leaf and the gray-green mix in the third leaf. Pull the veins with the curve of the leaf, beginning at the center and pulling toward either edge. Lift the brush as you pull the stroke to the edge so that the vein thins out and disappears before reaching the leaf edge. Thin the paint only enough to enable it to flow from the brush. Allow the veins to set up for a few minutes, then pull gently over them with the detail mop.

5 This illustration shows the final steps done in the second painting stage. The first stage must be completely dry before beginning this step. Apply a tiny amount of the Blending & Glazing Medium to the area. You may reinforce shading colors, as needed, with a brush side loaded in the original shading color used in the leaf or flower. You may strengthen the color tints or brighten the highlights. Remember that it takes very little paint when you are working over the dry first-stage painting.

You will also apply the violet centers in the second stage of the painting. An enlarged example with detailed instructions appears at right.

Add touches of the gray-green mix + the violet mix to the background. Apply this color here and there close to the leaves and flowers with a side-loaded ⅜-inch (10mm) or ½-inch (12mm) angle brush. Triangular spaces between two objects are a good place to use this color. Also apply it irregularly throughout the design to connect the white violet clusters and the purple violet design areas. Do not totally encapsulate the flowers and leaves and do not overdo the use of this background color. After applying, use your mini mop to soften the edges of this color into the china background or the previously applied dusty rose mix background.

Violet Center

Using the round detail brush, paint a tiny stroke of Cadmium Yellow Light + a pin dot of the dark red mix + a touch of the cream mix in the center of each violet. The fat portion of the stroke should rest on the lead petal, with the point pulling toward the back of the flower. This stroke should be so thin you will hardly do more than touch the tip of the brush down and pull slightly. Place a tiny amount of the dark red mix at the point of the stroke, pulling it out into the yellow just a bit. Rinse the brush and reload in the cream mix. Place two very tiny cream comma strokes on either side of the yellow stroke, overlapping the yellow slightly.

Painting the Purple Violet and Details

The following steps show the development of the purple violets, stems, calyx, filler fern and tendrils.

6 Basecoat the purple violets with a brush mixture of the violet mix + the red-violet mix, using the no. 2 flat brush. Vary this mixture so that all the petals and flowers aren't exactly the same. If you prefer, you may also paint some with the red-violet mix + the dusty rose mix. The coverage should be opaque, but avoid a heavy, ridged basecoat.

Shade the violet with the round detail brush and the dark violet mix + a touch of the dark red mix. After shading, blend the colors into the basecoat with a small angle brush.

7 Apply the highlights to the purple violets in the same manner that you applied them to the white violets. Use the round detail brush loaded in the cream mix + a pin dot of the violet or red-violet mix. We're adding the violet hues to the highlight to keep from building the bright values too quickly. After applying, soften slightly by pulling over the highlights with the detail mop.

8 Load the round detail brush in the dark violet mix or the dark violet mix + the dark red mix. Thin the paint slightly so that it flows easily from the brush. Apply streaks to all of the purple violet petals. Allow the streaks to set up for a few minutes, then soften by pulling over them with the detail mop.

9 This illustration shows the second stage of the painting. Be sure the first stage is totally dry before beginning this stage. Before painting, apply a small amount of Blending & Glazing Medium to each area. It will take even less paint when doing the overpainting steps.

As with the white violets, you may enhance any step done in the first painting: shading, color tints or highlights. If all the violets look exactly the same, you may wish to add tints of a hue not used in the first painting stage. Streaks may also be accented. Paint the violet centers exactly as you did in the white flowers. It will be a bit easier to see them in the violet flowers.

This illustration also shows the background color in place. Add the background color as you did for the previous steps, using a brush mixture of the gray-green mix + a touch of the violet mix. The filler ferns, stems and tendrils are much easier to paint with the background dry. If you need to make corrections to these elements, it is much easier on a dry background.

Add the filler ferns next. Thin some of the gray-green mix slightly with turpentine or paint thinner. Load the round detail brush in the thinned paint, wipe it and pull wispy stem strokes with the point of the brush.

On some of the wispy stems, paint tiny suggestions of fern leaves. To do so, lay the brush on the side of the point and make tiny strokes with a wiping motion, progressing down each side of the stem.

Add the stems and tendrils next, again using the round detail brush and slightly thinned paint. First use a brush mixture of the warm green mix + the gray-green mix. Wipe the brush and pick up a bit of the medium green mix + a touch of the black-green mix. Pull a bit of shading on the stems and tendrils where they move behind each other or another design element. Rinse the brush and load it with the cream mix + a touch of the warm green mix. Pull this mix over the areas that you wish to bring forward or on top of other areas.

Basecoat the calyx with the tiny no. 0 flat brush loaded with a mixture of the warm green mix + the gray-green mix. Wipe the brush and side load it with the medium green mix + a touch of the black-green mix. Pull this along one side of each calyx stroke. Wipe the brush and load it in the cream mix + a touch of the warm green mix. Stroke this color on the side of the calyx opposite the shading.

Finishing Your Project

When you've completed both sides of the mail holder, allow them to dry thoroughly. When dry, apply ten to twelve coats of a good quality spray varnish. I varnished mine with Blair Satin Tole. Before applying, shake the can vigorously for about one minute. Test spray on practice paper to be certain the can is spraying evenly. Hold the can as upright as possible, sixteen to eighteen inches from the surface. Apply the spray in light coats. Do not spray in extremely humid conditions, early morning or at night.

Magnolia Tray

Having grown up in the South, I consider the *Magnolia grandiflora* to be part of my heritage. In southern Texas and Louisiana, where I spent my childhood and most of my adult life, the trees attain a tremendous size. While living at Hope Villa plantation in Louisiana, I photographed and studied the magnolia extensively. One approximately 125-year-old tree on our property was nearly as large as the majestic live oaks surrounding it. The blossoms on the tree reached the proportions of a dinner plate and the leaves were sometimes ten inches long.

At every season the magnolia offers something of great beauty. Its leaves are a rich, glossy green with a velvety, brownish underside. They are a rather thick and rigid leaf, and are lovely for floral arrangements and decorations. The flowers are a creamy color with such a heavy scent they can be overpowering. Even the flower centers are beautiful: They open in the fall to reveal pockets containing vivid red seeds.

When painting this simple composition of one large blossom, two buds and surrounding leaves, I worked to capture the regal quality of the magnolia. The flower, though containing strong shading values, stands out as creamy white against the rich green of the leaves. The leaves contrast with the flower, and it is their strong values that determine those used throughout the remainder of the painting. The dramatic effect of the painting is achieved largely by the use of these strong, contrasting values.

With this design's strong contrasts and tight spatial composition, to avoid confusion, it is important to establish a dominant focal point—the large blossom—and to keep all other elements in a secondary position. The following factors help to achieve the center of interest:

Size and Placement—This blossom is the largest single element in the design and has a central location within the composition.

Value and Contrast—The blossom contains the brightest overall area within the painting. Within this flower, there is a broader range of values from lightest to darkest than on any other object. It also has great contrast with the surrounding leaves.

Color Temperature—There are more warmer hues contained within the blossom than in any other element. There are warm yellow tints on the petals and warm yellows and reds in the center.

Intensity—The colors in and around this focal point area are more intense than in the surrounding secondary leaves and buds.

It is also necessary to adjust these properties within the secondary objects surrounding the center of interest. Notice that the buds do not contain as many values or as great a contrast as the main blossom. They also have more cool color and are not as sharply detailed. The placement of the buds is not as predominant; they are tucked behind leaves. Finally, they do not occupy as much space as the larger blossom.

Although the leaves occupy a large amount of space within the composition, they are also secondary. The leaves are used to accent and call attention to the center of interest. They also contribute to the flow of the composition and aid in leading the eye of the viewer from one area to another.

MATERIALS

Palette

Winsor & Newton Finity Artists' Acrylics

- Burnt Umber
- Cadmium Yellow Medium
- Dioxazine Purple
- Gold Ochre
- Phthalo Blue Red Shade
- Red Iron Oxide
- Titanium White

Winsor & Newton Griffin Alkyds (for antiquing)

- Burnt Umber
- Dioxazine Purple
- Phthalo Blue

DecoArt Americana Acrylic Paints

- Desert Sand DA7
- Midnite Green DA84

Surface

This large, oval tray is available from Brenda Stewart by Design, 228 Yorkshire Dr., Williamsburg, VA 23185; phone (757) 564-7093.

Winsor & Newton Brushes

- Series 7 no. 1 Kolinsky sable round
- Series 240 no. 2 or no. 3 white mop (used for alkyd antiquing)
- Series 545 ½-inch (12mm) square comb
- Series 555 ½-inch (12mm) oval comb
- Series 560 ¼-inch (6mm), ⅜-inch (10mm), ½-inch (12mm) and ¾-inch (19mm) or 1-inch (25mm) synthetic angles
- Series 580 ⅛-inch (3mm) one-stroke lettering brush
- Series 740 no. 1 red sable liner brush
- Series 760 ¾-inch (19mm) red sable angle (used for alkyd antiquing)
- Series 5977 no. 1 or no. 3 hog bristle fan

Medium

- Winsor & Newton Acrylic Flow Improver, diluted mix
- Winsor & Newton Blending & Glazing Medium (used for alkyd antiquing)

COLOR MIXES

Cream Mix
Titanium White + a pin dot of Cadmium Yellow Medium + a pin dot of Gold Ochre

Pale Mocha Mix
cream mix + a touch of Gold Ochre + a touch of Burnt Umber

Medium Green Mix
Phthalo Blue Red Shade + Burnt Umber + a touch of Cadmium Yellow Medium + a touch of Gold Ochre + a pin dot of Dioxazine Purple

Dark Green Mix
medium green mix + a touch of Phthalo Blue Red Shade + a touch of Dioxazine Purple

Black-Green Mix
dark green mix + a touch of Burnt Umber + a touch of Phthalo Blue Red Shade + a touch of Dioxazine Purple

Dark Red Mix
Red Iron Oxide + a touch of Dioxazine Purple

Alkyd Antiquing Color
Phthalo Blue + Burnt Umber + a touch of Dioxazine Purple

This pattern may be hand-traced or photocopied for personal use only.
Enlarge at 186 percent to return to full size. The dotted line represents
the edge of the tray—for placement only.

Magnolia Tray

Preparation

Sand the tray and wipe thoroughly with a tack cloth. Seal both the front and back surfaces with a penetrating wood sealer. Allow the tray to dry for thirty minutes. Sand the tray lightly and wipe with a tack cloth.

Basecoat the painting surface of the tray with two coats of Desert Sand. Thin the paint with water to a strong value wash consistency. Allow time for complete drying between coats. When the final coat is dry, sand very lightly with Super Film ultra-fine grain sanding film.

Basecoat the back of the tray with Midnite Green. Two solid coats should adequately cover the surface. Add just enough water to the paint to obtain a flowing consistency. Allow for complete drying between coats. When the back of the tray is thoroughly dry, apply two coats of the same waterbase finish varnish to be used on the completed project. This will protect the dark color on the back of your tray. Dark-colored surfaces are very easily marred until varnished.

Place the magnolia pattern on the lower right curve of the tray. Use the dotted lines given for the edge of the tray to place the pattern. Using gray graphite paper, transfer the magnolia pattern to the tray. Transfer only the most necessary lines. These lines should be fine but clearly visible.

Painting Procedure

Begin the painting by basecoating the blossom and buds. While they are drying, apply the first basecoating steps to the leaves. The following pages show each element of the painting broken down into steps, making it easier to understand the development of the particular parts. However, you should develop different parts of your painting simultaneously. This will enable you to balance values and intensities as the painting progresses. For this reason, while you are waiting for the flowers to dry, apply the first basecoats to the predominant and secondary leaves and the stems.

After you have completed the basecoating steps, apply the first and second shading to the flowers, leaves and stems. Move from one area to the next to allow for drying time. Reapply the shading as many times as necessary to achieve the desired darkness within each element.

When the shading steps are complete, add soft value tints to the flowers and leaves. These tints should be very subtle and should only be visible for what they accomplish, rather than being noticeable as independent hues.

Next, paint the center of the flower. After painting the center, you may immediately see the need for stronger tints in the focal flower.

Now begin developing the background colors. Adding the background will help you see what color and value adjustments are needed in the flowers and leaves. It will also enable you to better balance the highlights that are still to be added.

After you've applied the background, develop the highlights in the flowers and leaves. Build these highlights gradually, highlighting each element only as much as necessary for its spatial position and importance.

Final adjustments should then be made throughout the painting—strengthen a dark here, a tint or perhaps a highlight there. Then strengthen the deeper background areas. At this time, look for areas that need to be "pulled out" or emphasized by adding additional dark around them. Also feed the dark from one area into the shadow points of another to push things into "atmosphere" and relieve the "cut-and-paste" look of your painting.

Now add the reddish brown stripe around the tray. I chose this color to balance the touches of reddish brown that are used in the flower center and flower and leaf tints. The red is important to establish interest and give visual relief in a painting that has so much of the dominant green hues.

The lines of magnolia leaves and blossoms are more rigid and have more strongly defined edges than many other flowers. For this reason, I added tendrils to soften the overall lines of the composition. Barely perceptible spattering done around the edges of the tray also helps to soften the composition.

To complete the tray, antique the outer perimeters. I did my antiquing with alkyds. You may also use oils or wide-floated acrylic color. Apply the color around the outer edges and fade it inward. The antiquing will also further subdue the leaves that are close to the edges of the tray.

Painting the Blossoms, Buds and Stems

1 Using the ½-inch (12mm) angle brush fully loaded with paint, basecoat the flower and buds solidly with the pale mocha mix. Pick up only enough water in the paint to obtain a flowing consistency. Two coats will be required to obtain a strong, even basecoat.

Basecoat all stems with the ¼-inch (6mm) angle brush loaded in a medium value wash of Burnt Umber + a touch of the dark green mix.

Next, shade the flowers with the ½-inch (12mm) angle brush, side loaded in the black-green mix. Prior to shading, dampen each area to be painted with clean water. Also apply a first shading to the stems with the ¼-inch (6mm) angle brush, side loaded in Burnt Umber + the black-green mix.

2 Dampen once again and deepen the flower shading with a brush side loaded in a stronger value of the black-green mix. This side load should be narrower in the brush than the previous shading value. Tuck this color into the deepest recesses of the shadows. Then, dampen the flower stems and add a bit of darker value to them with a smaller angle brush side loaded in the black-green mix + a touch of Burnt Umber.

Next, dampen one area of the flowers at a time and apply soft tint or accent hues. Side load these very softly into the ½-inch (12mm) angle brush. Use a very pale value of the dark red mix for the cool tint, adding it here and there in the lighter blending edges of shadows on both the blossom and the buds.

Apply the second, warmer tint mostly to the large blossom, with only a bit added to the upper bud. Dampen and apply in the warmer areas of the flower with a very pale value side load of Gold Ochre. These warmer areas may touch a soft blending edge of a shadow, but will usually be near the lighter areas.

3 The next step is to apply highlights to the flowers. Dampen the area to be painted and apply the cream mix with a side-loaded ½-inch (12mm) angle brush. If this first highlight application is too strong, skim over the area with a clean, damp brush. Apply the highlights to areas on the upper left of petals, or to brighten an edge.

Allow the first highlighting step to dry, then strengthen with another application of the cream mix. Apply the color in the same manner as the first highlight, but to a smaller area within the first highlight. The highlights should be stronger on the predominant, large blossom.

4 Begin painting the center of the flower by applying a medium value wash to both the upper and lower portions of the center. Apply this with a brush of an appropriate size, loaded in Gold Ochre. The wash does not have to be perfectly even, as only a bit of this undercoat will show through the completed center.

5 Dampen the upper portion of the center. With the point of a small round brush, dab in the dark green mix in a crescent shape, just off the edge of the right and lower curve of the oval. This color will "blossom" a bit due to the damp surface.

Side load the ¼-inch (6mm) brush with the dark red mix. Dampen the lower portion of the center and apply this color down the right side, under the upper portion of the center. Then carry it down the right side and across the lower edge. Also apply the dark red mix narrowly on the left edge. Notice how this shading moves across this section in an uneven, curved manner.

6 Dampen the upper portions of the center again. Add the reddish brown tint or accent. Tap in the dark red mixture to the inside of the crescent. This color should blossom as the shading color did.

Dampen the lower portion of the center and add a deeper shading under the upper portion, right off the right-hand edge and across the lower edge. Apply this with a narrow side load of the dark red mix + a touch of the black-green mix. This shading should stay within the first. It does not occupy as much space in this area.

7 With the point of a small round brush loaded in the dark red mix + a pin dot of the black-green mix, paint the tiny dark commas over the center. Begin at the top and work down, progressing from the outside edges in. When this is dry, apply highlight strokes of Cadmium Yellow Medium + a touch of Gold Ochre + the cream mix to the center. They may hit directly on or between the darker strokes. Mix a slightly brighter value of this color on the point of the brush by adding more cream to the mixture. With this value, build the highlight on the strokes toward the upper left of this section.

Dampen the lower portion of the center and tap in a bit of highlight just off the left edge. Use the highlight brush mixture of Cadmium Yellow Medium + a touch of Gold Ochre + a touch of the cream mix.

Painting the Leaves

The next six illustrations take you through the development of both the predominant and the secondary leaves.

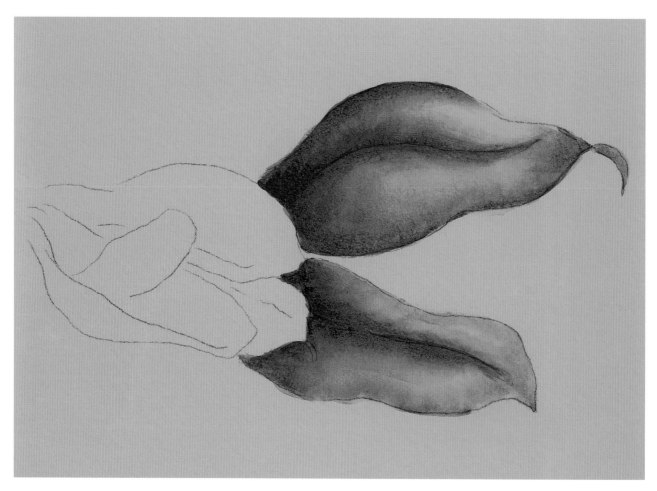

8 Basecoat the predominant leaves (the upper leaf in this illustration) with a side load of the medium green mix. Dampen the area to be worked and apply the paint with a ½-inch (12mm) or ¾-inch (19mm) angle brush. Do not attempt to apply all the areas of green that you see in the example in one step. Do as much as you can without beginning to lift an area that is damp. Basecoat areas of other predominant leaves while the first application is drying, then return to add more basecoat area to the dry leaf. This basecoat color normally begins at the back of the leaf, softens out into a curve and progresses along the darker side of the leaf. It may also be added curving along the lighter edge of the leaf. It may or may not be along all edges. It will normally curve back around the tip, filling the triangular space in this area. It is also in any dark shadow points and progresses down the center vein, soft-

ening on both sides. Be sure that it walks out to cover a sizable area of the leaf. If you do not move this color out extensively enough, it will be lost when you add shading values.

Basecoat any underside portions of leaves in a pale value of Burnt Umber + a touch of the dark green mix. Apply this with any brush that will cover the small area.

Basecoat the cooler, secondary leaves (the lower leaf in this illustration) in the same manner as the predominant leaf. A different color is used, and the values may not be as strong. On these leaves, the initial color is the dark green mix. Dampen these leaves and apply the color with a side-loaded ½-inch (12mm) or ¾-inch (19mm) angle brush. On the example, notice that the color moving along the edges and at the tip is much softer than on the predominant leaf.

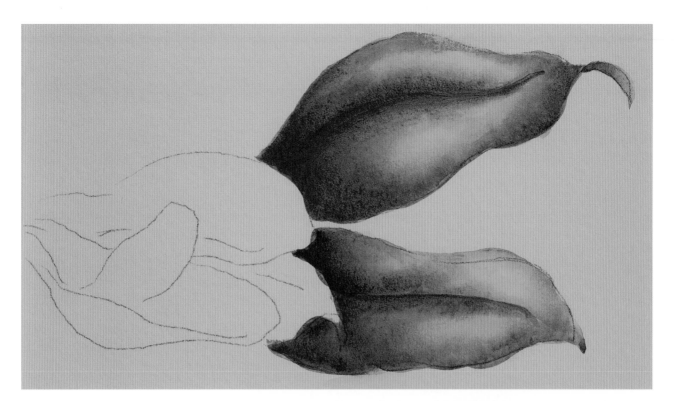

9 Next, apply the first shading color to the predominant leaves. Use the dark green mix, side loaded in the ½-inch (12mm) or ¾-inch (19mm) angle brush. Dampen the leaf prior to applying the shading color. Apply the shading value at the back of the leaf, in the shadow points, along the central vein, here and there along the edges and a bit at the tip. This value should not move out so far that it covers all the medium green basecoat color.

Shade any undersides of leaves with a brush mixture of Burnt Umber + the black-green mix. Side load the color into the ¼-inch (6mm) angle brush and apply to these areas.

Shade the secondary leaves with a slightly stronger value of the dark green mix. Apply this value to the shadow points, along the vein, and here and there along an edge. The shading of the secondary leaves will not become as strong as the shading on the predominant leaves. Keep this shading color in a smaller area, within the first basecoat color.

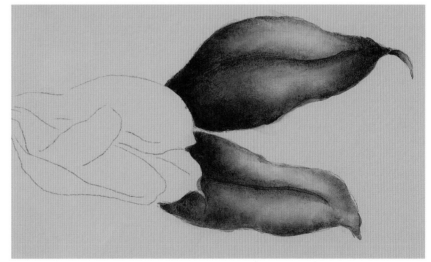

10 Reinforce the darkest areas of the leaves with deeper shading colors. Apply the colors as you did the initial shadings, on a damp ground with a side-loaded brush. They should stay within an area smaller than the first shading. On the predominant leaves, use the black-green mix. On the secondary leaves, use the dark green mix + a touch of the black-green mix. In the example, notice that the dark values of the secondary leaves are not as dark as those

of the predominant leaves.

Next, tint the leaves with subtle red accents. Apply the tints into a damp ground, with a side-loaded ½-inch (12mm) angle brush. Add these red tints at the softening edges of dark or medium areas. On the predominant leaves, use a pale value of the dark red mix. On the secondary leaves, use an even paler value of the dark red mix + a touch of the black-green mix.

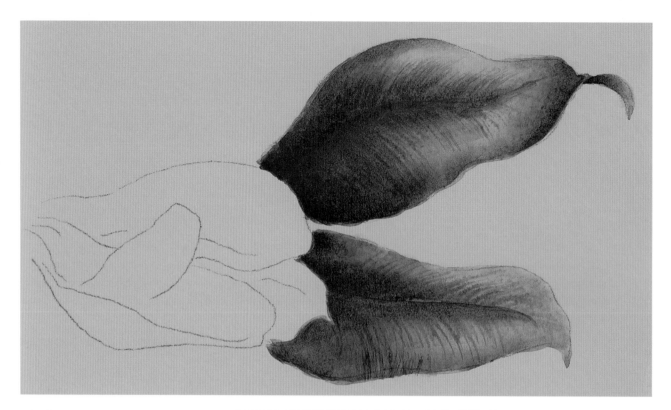

11 With the ½-inch (12mm) square comb brush loaded in the basecoat or shading green (whichever is appropriate for the area), pull from the vein outward on some of the leaves. When painting with the comb brush, it is necessary to thin the paint with water to a good flowing consistency. In order to obtain a slight softening of this color, skim the leaf with a damp brush prior to paint application. This color moves outward from the vein with the curvature of the leaf. Lift the brush as you pull outward, so that the color stops irregularly. Here and there, it may pull all the way to the outside edge of the leaf. Apply more of the combed color to the predominant than to the secondary leaves.

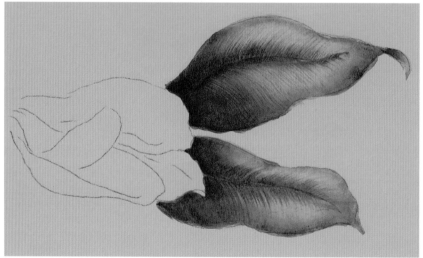

12 Highlight the predominant leaves with the ½-inch (12mm) oval comb brush. As you did in the previous step, skim the surface of the leaf with a damp brush before painting. This will soften the color slightly. Use a brush mixture of Cadmium Yellow Medium + a pin dot of the medium green mix + a touch of the cream mix. Apply these highlights by pulling from the outside of the highlight in toward the dark at the vein. Lift the brush as you move into the dark. The secondary leaves do not have any applied highlight.

13 Brighten the stronger highlights with a second application of color. For this brighter value, use more cream mix and Cadmium Yellow Medium mixed into the first highlight color. The brighter highlights occupy a smaller area within the original highlight. Prior to adding these, you may or may not need to dampen the surface.

With the point of the small round brush or the liner, apply a bit of light color along the vein. Use a brush mixture of Cadmium Yellow Medium + the medium green mix + the cream mix. Adjust the value of the color according to the area to which you are applying it. You do not want it to be extremely bright. Allow this step to dry. Wash over any shaded areas or areas that are too bright with a wash of the medium or dark green mix.

Painting the Background

The first of the following examples illustrates the painting of the background. In the second illustration, deeper background areas have been strengthened, and the stripe and background spattering have been added.

14 To paint the background, dampen an area larger than that of the background and set in the first color. Use a large ¾-inch (19mm) or 1-inch (25mm) angle brush. Side load it in a wide side load of the dark green mix. Set the color side of the brush next to the flowers and leaves and pat-stroke the color to walk it outward. As you can see in the illustration, the color is not perfectly smooth—it shows some soft stroke movement. The color is not applied in an even width all around the design. The strongest color will rest in the triangular-shaped areas formed by the elements in the design. Work by progressing from these triangular areas outward. Then fill in any other areas that are not taken care of by these progressions. You will not achieve all the background color with one painting. Do a portion, allow it to dry, dampen again, then add another area.

15 Reinforce the darkest areas of the background—mostly in triangular areas—with a narrower side load of the black-green mix. Dampen the background surface prior to painting.

Paint the narrow stripe around the tray with the dark red mix and the ⅛-inch (3mm) one-stroke lettering brush. Thin the paint in the brush to a flowing consistency. Paint the stripe in the indented area of the tray, where the slightly raised sides meet the floor of the tray. Prior to painting this stripe, you may wish to accent this indention with a soapstone pencil line or a very pale lead pencil line. This will serve as a guide

as the indention line is faint and not always easy to see from every angle.

When the stripe is dry, load a bristle fan brush with the dark green mix. Thin the paint a bit with water. Practice spattering on a test surface. You may use your fingernail or a palette knife pulled from side to side across the fan brush to create spatters. When you have the spattering technique perfected, dampen the tray with a very large brush and begin to spatter the green color into the damp surface. Work from the outside edges of the tray inward.

The first spatters will soften in the damp surface just a bit. If too much blossoming occurs, wipe the spatters away and allow the surface to dry for a moment and respatter. The drier the tray, the sharper the spatters. It does not bother me to have some spattering drift over the edges of objects. If too much spattering lands on flowers or leaves, use a damp brush and lift it quickly.

Allow the first spattering step to dry. Then repeat the entire process using the dark red mix + a touch of the black-green mix.

Painting the Tendrils

16 With the liner brush loaded in thinned Burnt Umber + a touch of the black-green mix, paint the tendrils. They should be free-flowing and graceful, with varying thickness. This is achieved by varying the pressure on the brush as you paint the tendril. Warm up on a practice surface until you have the proper paint consistency and the loose, flowing quality of the tendrils.

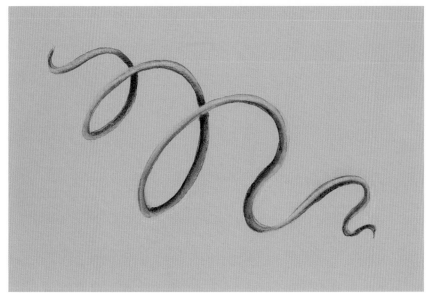

17 After the tendrils are dry, add shading with the liner brush loaded in a darker value of Burnt Umber + the black-green mix. Set the brush in the shaded area and pull out, lifting the brush as you pull. Also apply some narrower shading along the underside of the existing tendrils. Do this by painting the dark with less pressure, resulting in a narrower line. Allow this step to dry.

Apply a few highlights to upper curves of the tendrils. Use the liner brush loaded in Cadmium Yellow Medium + the medium green mix + the cream mix. Start the stroke prior to touching the brush to the surface so that you do not see a hard spot where you set the brush down. I refer to this as "getting a running start" on the stroke. Also, lift off the stroke at the end of the highlight area.

Adding the Antiquing

18 When you've completed the design, wipe the tray with a tack cloth, then apply one coat of the varnish to be used for finishing the project. Allow this to dry as directed. (If you'd prefer to antique the tray with floated acrylic color rather than alkyds, do not apply the coat of finish varnish. Skip to the instructions in sidebar.) With a small piece of lint-free towel, apply a scant coating of Winsor & Newton Blending & Glazing Medium to the top surface of the tray. Side load a ¾-inch (19mm) sable angle or flat brush with the alkyd antiquing mix. Blend the brush on the palette to soften the color and to widen the side load in the brush. Apply the side-loaded color around the perimeters of the painting surface. Apply the antiquing color over any design elements resting in this area.

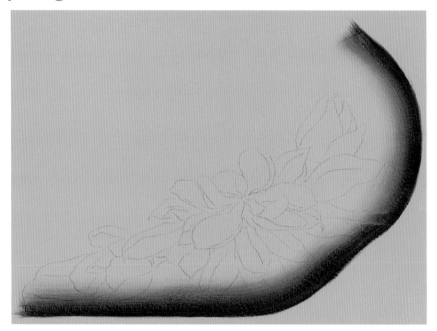

19 Mop the antiquing color to soften and move it out on the tray. The blending edges of the color should disappear into the background of the painting. Use the mop brush in two different ways to accomplish the softening. First, lightly pounce the brush on the surface, softening and distributing the color. Then, complete the mop blending by going over the entire surface with light, long, finishing strokes. To remove excess paint, wipe the mop brush frequently throughout the process.

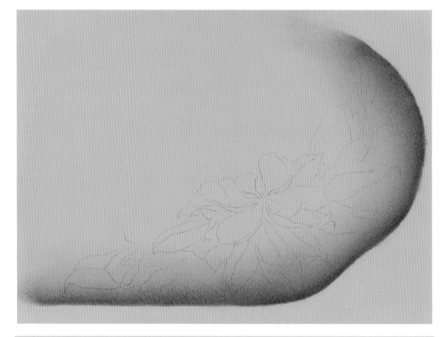

✖ *Tip* ✖

If you'd prefer to achieve the antiqued look with floated acrylic color, do not apply the coat of finish varnish. Dampen the surface with a very large brush, then apply a wide side-loaded float around the perimeters of the tray. You may use the dark green mix, the black-green mix or a brush mixture of the two. This step should be repeated several times with wide, soft values of paint, rather than attempting to accomplish the finished look in one step. When completed, the floats should closely resemble the alkyd antiquing shown in step nineteen.

Finishing Your Project

When the painting is complete, varnish the tray with a good quality waterbase varnish. Use a large, synthetic brush to apply six to ten coats. Allow to dry thoroughly and wipe with a tack cloth between coats. When the varnishing is complete, wax the piece with a coat of J.W. etc. Painter's Finishing Wax.

Magnolia Tray

Sonnet in Gray

The pattern on this teacup was inspired by an antique Aynsley cup, greatly simplified so that the painted cup has the same general feeling of the original cup, but is much easier to paint.

The interesting shape of the cup and the intricate pattern on the china were needed to add interest to this very simple composition. The linen also has an intricate embroidery and cutwork pattern. I repeated the china pattern motif at the top of the oval box for balance and color repetition. The drop of the box lid has a reprise of the china pattern and the deep box sides are accented with very soft sponging that repeats the colors in the painting. Thus the various box surfaces are unified with color and pattern repetition.

I designed this composition for a simple, nonintimidating introduction to painting still lifes. Although I painted the piece in acrylics, if you enjoy oil or alkyd painting, you might wish to do the china and linen patterns in acrylics, then proceed with the overall shading, tinting and highlighting with oil or alkyd glazes.

Preparation

Begin by sanding the box. Wipe thoroughly with a tack cloth. Seal all box surfaces with a penetrating wood sealer. Allow to dry for thirty minutes. Sand the box lightly and wipe with the tack cloth.

Basecoat the sides and the top of the box lid with two to three coats of acrylic. Use a mixture of 3 parts DecoArt Americana Titanium White + 1 part Light Buttermilk. Thin the paint with water to a flowing consistency. This will enable you to obtain a smoother, ridge-free basecoat. Allow the paint to dry completely between coats. When the final coat is dry, sand very lightly with Super Film ultra-fine grain sanding film.

Basecoat the drop of the lid, inside the lid, the box

MATERIALS

Palette

Winsor & Newton Finity Artists' Acrylics
- Burnt Umber
- Cadmium Yellow Medium
- Gold Ochre
- Naphthol Red Medium
- Naples Yellow
- Phthalo Blue Red Shade
- Renaissance Gold
- Titanium White

DecoArt Americana Acrylics
- Grey Sky DA111
- Light Buttermilk DA164
- Titanium White DA1

Surface

This oval, scalloped-edge box is available from Brenda Stewart by Design, 228 Yorkshire Dr., Williamsburg, VA 23185; phone (757) 564-7093.

Winsor & Newton Brushes
- Series 7 no. 0 or no. 1 Kolinsky sable round
- Series 500 no. 4, no. 6, no. 10 and no. 16 synthetic flats
- Series 560 ⅛-inch (3mm), ¼-inch (6mm), ⅜-inch (10mm), ½-inch (12mm) and ¾-inch (19mm) or 1-inch (25mm) synthetic angles
- Series 740 no. 0 or no. 1 red sable liner

Medium

Winsor & Newton Acrylic Flow Improver, diluted mix

Other
- Small natural sea sponge with medium texture
- Ruling pen

These patterns may be hand-traced or photocopied for personal use only. Enlarge at 161 percent to return to full size.

Lid drop design.

surfaces and the outer box bottom in Grey Sky. Follow the previous instructions to obtain an even, ridge-free basecoating.

Using gray graphite paper, transfer the still-life pattern to the box lid. Transfer only the most necessary lines. Do not apply the floral pattern to the teacup at this time. It will be applied after the gray basecoating is on the cup. Apply only the lines that define the gray area, and the other general pattern lines. The lines should be fine, but clearly visible. A very accurate pattern will make the painting easier.

Apply the floral pattern at an upper oval position on the box top. Again, transfer only the most necessary lines. Also apply the floral pattern on the drop of the lid. Place this pattern at each curved portion of the lid drop (refer to page 111 to assist with placing the design). There are five repeats of this pattern on the box lid.

After applying the flower pattern to the lid drop, fill in the remainder of the area with a very light diagonal grid. A simple way to do this is to cut a 4-inch (10cm) strip of posterboard that is ⅜-inch (1cm)

Burgundy Mix
Naphthol Red Medium +
Burnt Umber + a touch of
Phthalo Blue Red Shade

Rose Pink Mix
burgundy mix + Naphthol
Red Medium + Naples
Yellow + Titanium White

Cream Mix
Titanium White + a pin
dot of Naples Yellow

Dark Blue Mix
Phthalo Blue Red
Shade + Burnt Umber

Medium Blue Mix
dark blue mix + Phthalo
Blue Red Shade +
Titanium White

Leaf Green Mix
dark blue mix + Cadmium
Yellow Medium + a touch
of Naples Yellow + a
touch of Titanium White

Yellow-Green Mix
Cadmium Yellow
Medium + Naples
Yellow + a touch of leaf
green mix

Light Gray Mix
Titanium White + a pin
dot of dark blue mix + a
pin dot of Burnt Umber

Medium Gray Mix
light gray mix + a touch of
dark blue mix + a touch of
Burnt Umber

wide. Lay the strip at an approximate 45° angle and mark a light pencil line on either side. Position the strip very accurately against one pencil line and mark another line. Continue around the box, laying the strip accurately against one line and marking the next. When one direction has been completed, use the strip in the same manner to mark the opposing diagonal lines around the box.

Basecoat the gray areas on the cup and saucer with Grey Sky. Use a small flat brush that will fill the area comfortably and accurately. When the basecoating is dry, apply the small floral patterns to the cup. Use gray graphite paper and transfer only the most necessary lines. The grid pattern on the cup and saucer may be painted freehand, or you may apply the pattern as shown.

Painting Procedure

I have given you step-by-step instructions for painting the box sides and upper oval rose motif on page 110. The patterned portion of the cup and saucer is painted in the same manner, but lacks some of the detail. It is meant to be a mere suggestion of the china pattern. Do not work for perfection in this area. When first painted, it may look very predominant, but it will be subdued by shading and highlighting.

After completing the china pattern, basecoat the embroidery and cutwork pattern on the linen. Then apply shading around the embroidery design. This will give a raised effect to the pattern. Proceed with the shading, tinting and highlighting of the cup, saucer and linen. The color floating around the oval box top is added last. This soft floated color is important in that it acts as the frame of the painting surface.

When working on a multidimensional piece, there is normally a composition within another composition. For example, the still life on the upper box lid surface stands alone as a composition, with the teacup and saucer as the center of interest. But the entire box should also be treated as a composition, with the still-life area being the focal point. The pattern used on the drop of the lid might be too predominant on the same plane as the still life. But because the sides drop away from the focal point area, the design does not compete with nor overpower the primary subject matter.

Painting the Box Lid

Thnese three illustrations show the first steps in the development of the drop of the box lid. They will help you understand how to apply and develop the grid and how to place the floral motif around the box edges.

1 Basecoat the drop of the lid with Grey Sky. Allow to dry, then apply the floral pattern at each curved portion of the drop. Pattern the remaining area of the lid drop with a light diagonal grid, as instructed on page 101. Next, undercoat the rose, leaves, daisy centers and calyx with Titanium White acrylic. Using a small round brush, stroke on the daisy petals with the medium blue mix.

2 Apply fine gray lines to the grid pattern with a ruling pen and the medium gray mix + a touch of the dark blue mix + a touch of Burnt Umber. Keep scrap paper at hand to test for the proper consistency of paint and proper line width. Be certain to allow the lines in one direction to dry well before applying the lines in the opposite direction.

3 Load the ruling pen in the cream mix. Open the point of the ruling pen so that it will render a slightly wider line. Check the line width on your practice surface. Apply this slightly wider light line to the left of each gray line. Allow to dry. With the point of a small round brush, add a dot of the rose pink mix in the center of each diamond within the grid area. Allow these dots to dry thoroughly before continuing to paint on the lid drop.

Painting the Flower Design

 hese illustrations will take you through the steps in developing the floral design used around the lid drop and at the top of the oval on the lid surface. You will also use the instructions for painting the floral portion of the china design on the cup and saucer.

4 Load an appropriate-sized flat or angle brush with a pale value wash of the rose pink mix. Blot the brush and basecoat the rose with this pale pink wash. While the rose is drying, basecoat the leaves and daisy calyx in the same manner, using a pale value wash of the yellow-green mix. Basecoat the daisy centers with the ⅛-inch (3mm) angle brush, loaded in a pale value wash of Gold Ochre. When the rose is dry, add fine linework with a liner brush loaded in the burgundy mix.

5 Side load the ¼-inch (6mm) angle brush with a stronger value of the rose pink mixture than you used for the basecoat wash. This color will serve as the rose's medium value. Try to leave the original pale value in the lightest areas of the rose. Dampen the rose slightly with a clean brush, then apply this first shading with the brush side loaded with the rose pink mix. Apply the shading to the center of the rose, on the insides of the two lower, larger petals, then progress outward to loosely divide and define petals.

In the same manner, apply shading to the back and lower sides of the leaves and daisy calyx with a brush side loaded in the leaf green mix. Remember to dampen the leaves prior to shading. You may need to switch to a smaller brush for some of the leaves and the daisy calyx.

Shade around the lower curve of the flower centers with the ⅛-inch (3mm) angle brush side loaded in the burgundy mix + Burnt Umber. This area is very small, so predampening should not be required.

With a small round or liner brush and the dark blue mix, stroke darker blue shading on the daisy petals. Start the shading on the petal at the center of the flower. Lift the brush as you pull outward on the petal.

With the small round or liner brush loaded in the leaf green mix + the dark blue mix, paint the fern stems. With the same brush and color, apply the fern leaves with the point of the brush, making tiny press strokes.

6 Add a deeper value of shading to the rose with a brush side loaded in the burgundy mix. This darker value should occupy a smaller area than the first shading. Remember to predampen the surface as necessary. If darker linework is needed in the rose, add this with a liner brush loaded in the burgundy mix + a touch of the dark blue mix.

If darker shading is needed in the leaves, add this with the leaf green mix + a touch of the dark blue mix, applied with a side-loaded brush. If the brush you chose is large enough in proportion to the area you're painting, and if you blend your side load well, predampening of these small areas may not be needed.

Add fine linework to all leaves and the daisy calyx with the dark blue mix + a touch of the leaf green mix. Apply this to the rose leaf edges in a serrated manner. Also paint the center vein and a few very fine auxiliary veins with this mixture.

Pull a bit of highlight on the daisy petals with the cream mix + the medium blue mix. Use the small round or liner brush as you did when you applied the petal shading. Apply the color from the petal ends, lifting as you pull the brush toward the center.

7 If additional highlight is needed on the rose petals, paint this with the ⅛-inch (3mm) or ¼-inch (6mm) angle brush loaded in the cream mix + a touch of the rose pink mix. In order to keep the highlight from becoming too bright, dampen the rose before painting this step. These highlights should be applied primarily to the petal edges.

Line the daisy petals with the dark blue mix. This should be very fine and loosely applied. Also add a few tiny liner brush dots to the shaded area of the daisy centers with Burnt Umber + the burgundy mix.

Highlight the upper curve of the leaf veins with very fine lines of Renaissance Gold. Add small press stroke highlights of this color to the fern leaves. Also touch the daisy calyx and centers on the upper side with a bit of Renaissance Gold.

Painting the Still Life

The next six steps take you through the painting of the still-life composition. The cup and saucer are developed first, followed by the linen, background and foreground areas.

8 Basecoat the gray areas of the teacup and saucer with Grey Sky. When these are dry, apply the floral and grid patterns. Basecoat the roses, leaves, daisy centers and calyx with Titanium White acrylic. Use a small round brush to base the daisy petals with strokes of the medium blue mix.

With your ruling pen set to create a very fine line, apply dark lines to the grid pattern with the medium gray mix + a touch of the dark blue mix + a touch of Burnt Umber.

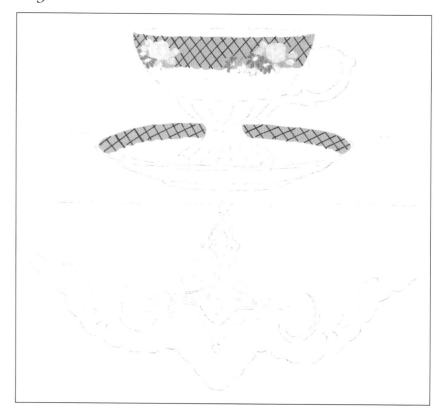

9 With the ruling pen set to create a slightly wider line, apply the lighter cream mix lines to the left of each dark gray line. Add the tiny pink dots to the center of each diamond in the grid area using the tip of a small round brush and the rose pink mixture. Allow the dots to dry thoroughly before continuing with successive steps.

Paint the gold rims and accents on the cup and saucer with a liner brush and Renaissance Gold. Add a very fine shading line of medium gray mix + a touch of the dark blue mix + a touch of Burnt Umber under the gold scallops at the lower edge of the gray areas.

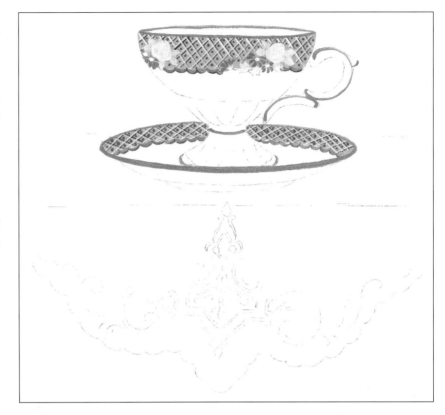

10 Next, paint the china floral designs. Do this in a manner similar to the floral design on the lid drop, deleting some detail. Remember that these elements are meant to merely suggest the china pattern. They are too small to need all the steps, and they will be somewhat concealed by the cup shading and highlighting steps.

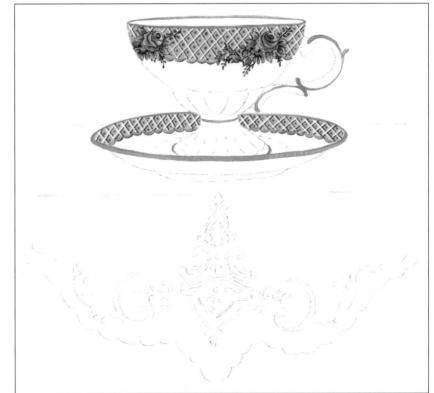

11 Add the first shading to the teacup and saucer with a ½-inch (12mm) angle brush side loaded in the light gray mix. Add the shading to one section of the cup and saucer at a time, dampening each area just prior to shading. Apply the shading to the small inside bowl area of the cup, placing it against the gold rim on the front outer bowl area. Next, work on the larger outer bowl area. Apply a shadow coming down the right side of the cup, curving across the bottom of this section and up the left side. The shadow should be wider on the right side of the bowl. This shading value extends all the way to the cup edges. It will not show very much on the gray area at the upper edge of the teacup. Because it will be left on the edge as the reflected light, it should be applied over the gray basecoat in this section.

Continue down to the lower scalloped section of the bowl. There are five sections to this portion of the cup. On the segments to the right of the center section, apply the shading to the right of the division lines and fill the lower point of each area. On this side of the cup, this value is relatively wide and may almost completely fill these sections. To the left of the center section, apply the shading to the left of the division lines and at the lower point of each area. The shading on this side of the cup is narrower. On the center segment of this area, apply this shading across the lower curve, then up the right side (staying just off the edge of the section), and back across the top for a short distance.

On the pedestal section of the cup, first apply the shading to the upper pedestal, not quite touching the section above. Dampen and stroke this on with the point of a round brush. Begin near the left edge with relatively short strokes. As you progress across to the right, lengthen the strokes. The last few strokes form the shadow running all the way down the right side of the pedestal.

Allow the previous steps to dry, then add the shading that forms the indentations on the pedestal. Dampen the area slightly and stroke under each curve

(showing on the right and left sides), then pull upward into the indentation.

Also shade the handle with the round brush. Dampen each area slightly and then pull the light gray mix shading to the inside or lower edge of the curves. Also apply this color to the two areas where the handle touches the cup.

Apply the same light gray mix to the saucer. Once again, dampen each area prior to applying the shading. On the inside of the saucer, the shadow rests on the lower edge, against the outside section of the saucer. Also apply this color around the elliptical shape in the center of the saucer. Do not attempt to shade under the gold rim or over the gray in the ends of the ellipse in this section—this color is too close to the basecoat value of these areas. We'll apply the shading to these areas with the darker value.

On the outer portions of the saucer, you may continue painting this value with a side-loaded brush, or you may switch to a round brush. In either case,

dampen the area prior to shading. On the larger section, apply the shading under the upper gold rim. The shading should be narrower on the left side of the saucer and should broaden on the right, covering almost the entire section on this side. On the lower, narrow base of the saucer, paint the shading to the upper side, against the previously painted section.

Paint the cutwork areas of the linen with a liner or small round brush and the medium gray mix + a touch of the dark blue mix + a touch of Burnt Umber. Apply the embroidery design with the liner or small round brush and the light gray mix. Allow these areas to dry.

Next, apply a darker value to the left and/or under the embroidery design with the medium gray mix. Dampen the area very slightly. Stroke this shading on with the liner or small round brush. It should soften slightly because of the damp ground. Also apply the shading just inside the outer embroidered edge of the linen.

12 Now apply a darker shading to the cup and saucer with the medium gray mix. Use the same combination of dampening, side loading and round brush techniques you used to apply the previous value. Apply this value to the same areas as the previous shading, but stay within the lighter value, occupying a smaller area than the first shading. Notice that this value stays away from rounded edges, leaving the first value showing.

Also use the darker value to set some shadows on the gray areas of the saucer that would not have been discernible if applied with the light gray mix. On the inside of the cup, these additional shadows are at the outer "corners" of the ellipse, under the gold rim at the outer saucer edge and against the pedestal of the cup.

Apply warm tints or accents to the cup and saucer with a very pale brush mixture of the cream mix + a pin dot of Naples Yellow + a pin dot of the rose pink mix. Predampen each area prior to applying the tint. Side load the color into an appropriate-sized angle or flat brush so that a portion of the brush will aid in the blending of the color into the surrounding area.

Add the tint color just inside the curved, blended edges of the shadows as they soften out into lighter areas.

Shade the gold areas of the cup and saucer next. Use a liner or small round brush loaded in the burgundy mix + Burnt Umber. Shade these areas on the lower side of each band, rim or scallop, leaving the shadings sharp and linear.

With a larger angle or flat brush side loaded in the light gray mix + a touch of the medium gray mix, apply shading to the linen under the cup and saucer. Dampen each section prior to applying the color. Begin with the flat surface under the cup, extending the shading out on either side of the cup, but broader on the right. Leave a small space of light to give the illusion of a table edge at the lower portion of this section. The line in the pattern will be taken into the shading in the drop of the cloth.

Now dampen the drop portion of the linen. Paint a shadow against the pattern line at the upper edge of this section. Apply the color from left to right. As you approach the right side of the area, work the shading down further into the linen. Then add a few soft, curved, diagonal sweeps across the cloth.

13 Apply highlights to the cup and saucer with a round brush and the cream mix + a pin dot of Cadmium Yellow Medium. Because a slight softening of these highlights is desired, dampen each area prior to application. Highlight the outer bowl of the cup very strongly toward the left side. Give the inner bowl a softer highlight on the right side, diagonally across from the previous highlight and just under the gold rim. Highlight the scalloped section of the bowl and the pedestal slightly inward from the left side. Add a stroke of highlight value on the upper curved section of the handle, just inside the gold stroke. Touch a highlight on the saucer over the gray on the left. Stroke the strongest highlight over the gray on the right side, slightly under the gold rim.

Now add sparkle to the gold rims with the liner brush loaded in Cadmium Yellow Medium + the cream mix. This value is a deeper yellow than the mix you used on the white areas of the cup and saucer. You may add a bit of sparkle here and there all along the gold accents, but the strongest sparkle should correspond with the highlight areas of the cup and saucer.

Paint the resting shadow under the saucer. The shadow forms an elliptical shape on the right side of the saucer and thins down as it moves under the saucer toward the left. It is darker next to the saucer and softens as it moves outward. Dampen the area and apply the resting shadow with a medium-sized angle or flat brush, side loaded in the medium gray mix. Darken the portion of the shadow touching the saucer with the medium gray mix + a touch of the dark blue mix + a touch of Burnt Umber.

Add a bit of warm tint or accent to the linen with a larger angle or flat brush side loaded with a brush mixture of the cream mix + a pin dot of Naples Yellow + a pin dot of the rose pink mix. Dampen the entire linen. Touch the tint color here and there, at the blending edges of shadows as they are softening into the lighter areas.

Highlights may be needed on the left tabletop surface or on the table edge. Apply this in a damp ground with a round brush. Use the straight cream mix for this highlighting.

Add soft background color at the upper portion of the composition next. This color should be heavier and extend out farther on the right of the cup and saucer, and should stay within the triangle formed by the cup and saucer on the left side. Dampen the entire background area, dampening farther out than you will apply color. Side load the ¾-inch (19mm) or 1-inch (25mm) angle brush with a brush mixture of the light gray mix + a touch of the medium gray mix. Blend this very carefully on the palette. Set the color side of the brush against the cup and saucer and work from the dark outward, allowing the blended side of the brush and the dampness of the ground to aid you in blending and losing color edges. Walk the color out in an irregular manner until edges are softened. Allow this to dry and repeat as many times as necessary to obtain the correct value and size of the background.

Shade the area under the linen in the same manner. Dampen and side load very carefully as instructed in the previous step. Use a brush mix of the medium and light gray mixes, mixed a bit darker this time. Place the color side of the brush against the linen, walking the color downward. The color should be somewhat darker and lighter on the right. Allow this to dry.

Dampen the area under the linen again. Set in a darker and very narrow shadow of the medium gray mix + a touch of the dark blue mix + a touch of Burnt Umber next to the linen. This shadow should be darker and a bit wider on the right side of the design and narrower and lighter on the left side.

Paint the floral design at the top of the oval as instructed for the floral motifs on the lid drop. Next, add a float of the light gray mix + the medium gray mix around the edge of the oval. Use the 1-inch (25mm) angle brush, side loaded and blended carefully on the palette. Dampen the box top to give extra time to complete the float all around the top. This floated color acts as a frame, helping to hold the eye of the viewer in the painting.

Painting the Lower Box Sides

These last four steps show the treatment used on the lower box sides. Because of the busy treatment on the lid drop and the depth of the box bottom, I used a rather simple treatment here.

14 Immerse a small sea sponge in clean water. Squeeze tightly to remove excess water; the sponge should be damp. Load one area of the sponge in the rose pink mixture. Tap on the palette to soften the load. Dampen the box sides slightly with clean water. Apply a soft application of the rose pink mix by pouncing the loaded sponge lightly on the box. Don't turn the sponge while it is touching the surface. If an area is too strong, quickly pounce over it with the unloaded back portion of the sponge. Allow to dry.

15 Rinse the sponge and squeeze it until it is just damp again. Load it lightly in the light gray mixture. Tap on the palette to soften the load, then tip a small edge of the sponge in a tiny amount of the medium blue mix. Tap on the palette to soften. Sponge the box sides again, using the same technique used for the pink sponging. Allow to dry. Mark a very pale pencil or chalk line 1″ (3cm) from the box bottom.

16 Rinse the sponge and squeeze until just damp. Load very lightly in Renaissance Gold. Apply a very pale sponging to the box sides. Allow this step to dry. Load a round brush with Grey Sky. Apply the comma stroke border on the line you marked 1″ (3cm) from the box bottom.

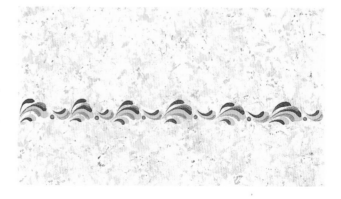

17 Add smaller accent commas to the border. Use the round brush loaded in the medium gray mix + a touch of the dark blue mix + a touch of Burnt Umber. When these strokes are dry, add a final accent with small Renaissance Gold comma strokes.

Apply rose pink dots to the border. Apply these with the point of a round brush. Allow them to dry thoroughly, then top with a smaller Renaissance Gold dot.

Finishing Your Project

When all painting is completed, varnish your piece with a good quality waterbase varnish. Use a large, synthetic brush to apply six to ten coats. Allow to dry thoroughly and wipe with a tack cloth between coats. When the varnishing is completed, the piece should be waxed with a coat of J.W. etc. Painter's Finishing Wax.

The inside of the box may be painted and decorated with complementary sponging or spattering. Some painters even like to add a small repeat of a portion of the design. The rose pattern on the upper box top could be repeated inside the box lid. If the box is to be a gift, it's nice to add the name or initials of the recipient. I have also added short brush-lettered notes or quotes inside box lids. If a complementary fabric can be found, you may wish to line the lower box section.

Sonnet in Gray

Flow Blue and Daffodils

affodils are one of the first signs of spring. If I'm lucky in my travel schedule, I'm able to see them in their peak bloom here in Virginia, and also in other locations where they bloom earlier or later. Daffodils were the perfect flower to fill the little antique blue pitcher that resides in my kitchen. The yellow "trumpet" section of the daffodils provides the touch of contrasting color needed to give this composition a dramatic center of interest.

The strong vertical composition I used in this painting is softened by the curves and flow of the flowers and leaves. The curved lines of the pitcher, the many curved lines in the china design and the curved lines in the embroidery and edge of the linen give balance through repetition of line within the design.

Gray-blue is the dominant color; I used it in slightly differing hues and values throughout the painting. I used very subdued and low intensity blue-gray in the background and for shading in the linen, pitcher and white flower petals. I used stronger values as shading in the leaves. This repeated color helps to establish color harmony within the composition. I used a more intensely blue version of this color on the china design, which is nearer the center of interest.

I used strong contrast, detail and the vivid yellow trumpet of the lower flower to pull the eye of the viewer into the painting and to help create the center of interest. I made the flower directly behind the bottom daffodil slightly softer in value and cooled down the yellow trumpet a bit more with the pale blue-gray. The upper flower has the least amount of contrast, and I touched it with more cool color than either of the lower blossoms. It is important to keep this relationship between the flowers if you are to establish a

MATERIALS

Palette

Winsor & Newton Artists' Water Colours
- Burnt Umber
- Cadmium Yellow Pale
- Gold Ochre
- Oxide of Chromium
- Permanent Alizarin Crimson
- Sepia
- Winsor Blue Red Shade

Winsor & Newton Designers' Gouache
- Bleedproof White

Surface

One-half sheet of 140-lb. (300gsm), 260-lb. (550gsm) or 300-lb. (638gsm) cold-press watercolor paper

Winsor & Newton Brushes
- Series 7 no. 1 Kolinsky sable watercolor round
- Series 550 no. 4 synthetic filbert
- Series 575 ½-inch (12mm) and 1-inch (25mm) synthetic oval filbert mops
- Series 720 no. 6 or no. 8 (medium) and no. 10 or no. 12 (large) red sable rounds
- Series 965 1-inch (25mm) or 1½-inch (38mm) synthetic and natural hair blend wash brush
- Series 5977 no. 1 or no. 3 hog bristle fan brush

strong center of interest.

Before you actually begin to paint, read the introduction to watercolor on page 22. It's important that you experiment with the colors on your palette. Refer to the color guides for each area in the project instructions. Brush mix the colors and test them on scraps of watercolor paper. You need to experiment with both the hue and the value of the various brush mixtures. It's also good to keep the test paper handy for testing hues and values as you develop the painting. You may wish to mix small puddles of some of the mixtures that are used in many areas of the painting— do this in one of the mixing wells on your palette.

If you don't wish to work in watercolor, try this painting in acrylic. It could be done on any suitable surface, basecoated in an off-white acrylic. The acrylic painting would be done in the same manner as the previous project, "Sonnet in Gray."

Preparation

Tape the pattern to the *back* side of a half sheet of watercolor paper. Place the paper on a lightbox and trace the pattern lines with a finely pointed HB drawing pencil. (If you don't have a lightbox, place the paper on a glass tabletop with a lamp beneath, or tape it to a window so that the sunlight shines through the paper, revealing the pattern lines.) Trace only the lines that are necessary for you to complete the painting. The lines should be very fine, but clearly visible. Next, securely tape all four sides of the watercolor paper to your work board.

This pattern may be hand-traced or photocopied for personal use only.
Enlarge at 181 percent to return to full size.

Painting Procedure

In the following pages, each section of the painting is shown from first step to completion. I believe this best enables you to see the development of the various compositional elements. The actual painting order is done a bit differently and may be varied quite a bit according to conditions during your painting sessions, such as the amount of time that you have to dedicate to a work session and the condition of the painting itself. Has the area become too set up to apply all steps listed for that painting stage? Do you have a troublesome area that will best be left alone for awhile to avoid overworking? Sometimes, you are simply tired of, or bored with, working in a particular area. This can cause you to do less than your best work. In any case, you need to see all the areas of the painting develop, little by little, simultaneously. Feel free to develop the painting in the manner that is most logical and easiest for you.

When I developed this painting, I began with the first two steps of the background and then progressed to the first stages of the pitcher and linen. I then added the first stages of the flowers and leaves. The successive steps were then added to the linen and pitcher, and then the flowers and leaves.

At this stage, you are able to see what additions—such as stronger values, color accents or tints—are needed in the various parts of the composition. Until you bring all the various elements of the composition to a certain stage, you are unable to determine these necessary additions. You may need stronger values to bring out the center of interest, or you may need to feed color from one area of the painting into another to create an illusion of space and to avoid a "cut-and-paste" look within the composition. It is now that you may see the need for a touch of warmer color in the cooler areas of the painting, such as the background, pitcher, linen or white flower petals. Or you may need to add cooler tones to the warmer trumpet areas of the flowers. The final touches to the painting are crucial to establishing color unity and spatial illusions.

There is no absolute right way to develop this painting. No painting will look exactly the same as another, nor do I feel we should desire "cookie-cutter" paintings. Different is not wrong. However, if your painting becomes so different that you feel it looks wrong, adjustments can always be made. Relax and enjoy the painting.

When the instructions do not state a specific brush size, use the size you are most comfortable with, and the one that best fits the area you are painting.

BACKGROUND COLOR MIXES

Winsor Blue Red Shade + Sepia (mixed to a blue-gray hue)

Winsor Blue Red Shade + Sepia (mixed to a neutral gray hue)

Sepia + Burnt Umber

Painting the Background

2 If the background color is still workable, you may drop stronger values into the background (skip to the next paragraph if the background has dried or set up too much). Use a brush mix of the Winsor Blue Red Shade + Sepia again, this time making the color a little more neutral, showing less blue (refer to the second swatch of the color mixing guide). Use the round brush again, loaded in stronger pigment. Blot the brush more thoroughly than you did for the first color application. Apply stronger touches to the right of the pitcher and flowers and just a bit to the lower left of the pitcher and under the linen. This value should occupy less space than the first background color.

If the background has set up too much, the second value may be applied in a separate step. Allow the first step to thoroughly dry, then wet the background area again with clean water, using less water than in the first application. Proceed as instructed in the paragraph above. It's not a bad idea to apply the background colors in two separate steps if you're inexperienced in watercolor or tend to overwork your painting.

1 Use the large wash brush to carefully apply clean water to the paper, working around the pitcher, linen, flowers and leaves. Use a small filbert or round brush to wet the smaller areas between leaves, flowers and the pitcher handle. Work the water into the paper by brushing repeatedly with the wash brush. The aim is to get the paper wet enough that you can complete the first two color steps before it dries.

First apply a medium value of Winsor Blue Red Shade + Sepia. As shown on the color mixing guide, the resulting gray should lean a little to the blue side. Apply this color into the damp ground with a large round brush. After loading the brush, blot lightly on a pad of paper

towels. As you can see, the color is not evenly applied. It is somewhat darker to the right side of the pitcher and under the linen and fades to the left.

Use the flat wash brush to soften, distribute or guide the background color as needed. The brush should be blotted and squeezed so that moisture is not introduced to the painted area.

Should the paper begin to dry as you are applying the first background color, apply water to an area beyond where you are working with the wet, blotted wash brush. Gradually work the water back toward the area where paint has been applied. This technique is referred to as "introducing water to an area."

3 In this step you'll add warmer tints to the background. The need for these warmer colors may not become apparent until your entire painting has progressed through several stages. Apply these tints into a slightly damp ground. Use the round brush loaded in a pale value of Sepia + Burnt Umber, then soften with a blotted and squeezed wash brush.

4 In one of the final stages of the painting, soft spattering is added to the background. I usually add this as the very last step, as I like for a bit of spattering to fall on the flowers and leaves.

Be certain that all areas are thoroughly dry. Dampen the background with the large wash brush. Whisk gently over the other painted areas with the damp brush—this will enable you to more easily lift spatters off areas where you don't want them. It will also help to soften the spatters on the areas where they are desirable.

Load the large hog bristle fan brush in a very dilute mixture of Winsor Blue Red Shade + Sepia. Blot the brush to remove excess paint. Pull a small palette knife across the bristles to spatter. Work from the outer edges of the painting, moving inward until you have spattered the desired areas. Repeat with a mixture of Sepia + Burnt Umber. With a clean blotted brush, remove any undesirable spattering.

Painting the Pitcher

5 Although I've outlined the shading steps for the pitcher below, you may move from area to area in a manner that will enable you to easily accomplish the shading. If you tend to overwork or overwet the paper, do not work two steps in the same area consecutively; allow the area to dry between steps and redampen.

Load a medium-sized round brush in a medium value mixture of Sepia + Winsor Blue Red Shade. Without wetting the paper, apply this color to the shaded areas on the upper right side of the pitcher. Work only about half of the pitcher at a time. Use a damp, blotted ½-inch (12mm) filbert to soften the edges of the color into the background. Approaching from the outside edge of the color, reach into and grab just the edge of the color and soften outward. Do not overwork. Some crisp edges are nice on the glazed china surface.

Next, apply this same color to the remainder of the upper pitcher section. Soften as instructed in the previous paragraph.

While this is drying, apply the shading color to the bottom section of the pitcher base. The shading should follow the upper edge of this segment. Soften the lower edge of the color by pulling along it with a damp, blotted filbert.

Work on the pitcher handle while the

previous section is drying. Continuing to work with the same color in the round brush, paint one or two areas of the handle shading. Immediately soften these with the damp, blotted filbert. Then add one or two more shaded areas, softening after each addition. If this small area becomes too wet to work successfully, allow it to dry before completing the shading.

Now paint the shadow on the segment above the base section. Apply the color directly under the curved line at the top of this segment. Make the shading wider on the right side of the pitcher, narrowing it as it moves toward the left. Soften the lower edge of this color by dragging along it with the damp, blotted filbert.

PITCHER COLOR MIXES

Winsor Blue Red Shade + Sepia

Sepia + Burnt Umber

Burnt Umber + Gold Ochre

Winsor Blue Red Shade + a touch of Sepia + a pin dot of Permanent Alizarin Crimson

6 You will now add deeper shading to the pitcher, using a stronger value of the same brush mix of Sepia + Winsor Blue Red Shade. Starting on a dry ground, apply this color with the round brush and soften with the damp, blotted filbert.

Apply the color in a smaller area along the right edge, and continue under the thickness of the upper pitcher edge. Also add it to the underside of the pitcher body, the upper edges of the base and to the handle. This value should always occupy a smaller area than the previous shading color.

After the deeper shading is applied and has been allowed to dry, apply warm tints to the pitcher. Do not wet the area. Apply the first of these tints to the warmer edges of the shaded areas, using a pale mixture of Sepia + Burnt Umber and an appropriately sized round sable brush. Soften with a damp, blotted filbert. Allow these tints to dry before proceeding.

Next, load the round brush in a very pale value mix of Burnt Umber + Gold Ochre. Apply this color in the very warmest areas of the pitcher, overlapping it into the softened shadows. Immediately soften by wiping over the area with a damp, blotted wash brush.

7 The outlines of the blue china pattern are applied next. The paper must be dry for this step. Thin a mix of Winsor Blue Red Shade + a touch of Sepia + a pin dot of Permanent Alizarin Crimson to a good flowing consistency (in order to obtain fine lines). Apply the outlines with an appropriate-sized round sable detail brush, slowing the speed of the brushstrokes to allow for the texture of the paper. The pattern is a good guide for the linework. Allow these lines to dry and cure for a short time.

Load a medium value of the same blue mixture into an appropriate-sized round sable brush. Apply suggestions of shading to the predominant areas of the china pattern with this color. Apply the color to a dry ground, then soften with a damp, blotted filbert. Use a light touch so that the linework is not disturbed.

Use a very diluted value of this color and fill in the smaller, less predominant leaves within the design. You are not looking for perfection in this china design. It is just a suggestion, and will be partly covered with the applied highlights.

8 Highlights are now applied to the pitcher with Bleedproof White. Load an appropriate-sized round sable brush with the Bleedproof White. The consistency should be thin enough for the paint to flow, but not overly thin. Apply the shine areas to the pitcher on a dry ground. Immediately skim over the shine areas lightly with a damp, blotted wash brush. They should be softened very minimally.

Painting the Linen

9 The first step on the linen is to apply color to the embroidery design. Apply this with the point of an appropriate-sized round sable brush loaded in a very pale value of Winsor Blue Red Shade + Sepia. The paper should be dry when this is applied.

10 Next, paint a narrow shadow next to the embroidery with a stronger value of the Winsor Blue Red Shade + Sepia mixture. On the inner design work, it is painted mostly to the left and under the embroidery elements. Here and there, you will need a touch on the right side also to give a raised look to the embroidery. Apply this to a dry ground. At the outer edge of the linen, the shadow line is placed inside the scalloped edge. After this dries, dampen inside the scalloped edge and apply the color again, so that a softer shading is also seen in this area.

LINEN COLOR MIXES

Winsor Blue Red Shade + Sepia (pale value)

Winsor Blue Red Shade + Sepia (stronger value)

Burnt Umber + Gold Ochre

11 Dampen the linen from a point approximately ¼-inch (6mm) below the table line to the lower edge of the fabric. With an appropriate-sized round sable brush loaded in a medium value of Winsor Blue Red Shade + Sepia, apply the shading to the linen. It extends all the way across the linen, underneath the imaginary line where you dampened. On the right side of the linen, stroke the color downward with the side of the round brush. As the shading color moves downward, swing it across the fabric from right to left in a few slightly curved movements.

Next, dampen the tabletop area of the linen. Dampen from the table line upward, working around the pitcher. Apply very pale color to the right of the pitcher and then stronger color to the left of the pitcher. Also apply a bit of stronger color against the table line. This is a bit stronger and wider on the right side. Allow this to dry.

You are now left with a small space of light that creates the edge of the table. Since the linen is not sharply creased on the table edge, this line must be softened. Use the damp, blotted 1-inch (25mm) wash brush and gently scrub the inner sharp edges of this area until it softens ever so slightly.

12 Strengthen the shading as needed on the linen, using a stronger value of the Winsor Blue Red Shade + Sepia mix. Apply the stronger shadows on a dry ground and soften by skimming over them with a damp wash brush.

Warm tints are added to the linen using a very pale value of a Burnt Umber + Gold Ochre mix. Dampen the linen with a wash brush and apply the warm tints at the softening edges of a few of the shadows. Use an appropriate-sized round sable, blotted brush. If additional softening is needed, quickly skim over the area with a damp, blotted wash brush.

Paint a strong resting shadow on the linen under the pitcher. It should be wider on the right and narrow toward the left side of the pitcher. Give the shadow a slight elliptical shape as it wraps around the right side of the pitcher. Apply this shadow on a dry ground, using a medium strong value of Winsor Blue Red Shade + Sepia. Soften the blending edge slightly with a damp, blotted filbert. Soften the color in place, being careful not to distort the shape or move the color too far outward.

Painting the Flowers

13 Load an appropriate-sized round sable brush in Cadmium Yellow Pale + a touch of Gold Ochre. Apply color to the dark and medium areas of the flower trumpets. Apply the color to a dry ground, then soften the blending edges of the applied color with a small, blotted filbert brush. If too much light is covered, lift some light back into the flowers with the damp, blotted filbert.

Apply shading to the outer flower petals with a medium value brush mix of Winsor Blue Red Shade + Sepia. Apply the shading where petals overlap each other and close to the yellow trumpet areas. Also use the shading color to create pleats and flips. This color can also be applied softly to outer petal edges to contour the leaves. Apply on a dry ground, using an appropriate-sized round sable brush. Soften with the damp, blotted filbert. Allow to dry. With a pale value of this mix in an appropriate-sized round sable brush, paint soft streaking on the front flower, and here and there on the flower just behind this one. Do not apply any streaks to the upper flower.

Load the ½-inch (12mm) filbert mop with a very pale value of Oxide of Chromium. Basecoat the six most predominant leaves in the painting with this color. Next, load the filbert with a pale value of Oxide of Chromium + Winsor Blue Red Shade + a touch of Sepia. Basecoat the remaining, cooler leaves in the painting. As you are simply filling in areas, these colors are applied to a dry ground.

FLOWER COLOR MIXES

Cadmium Yellow Pale + a touch of Gold Ochre

Gold Ochre + Permanent Alizarin Crimson + Burnt Umber

Permanent Alizarin Crimson + Burnt Umber

Winsor Blue Red Shade + Sepia

14 Next, use Gold Ochre and an appropriate-sized round sable brush to add a slightly darker value to the throat of the yellow trumpet portion of the daffodils. Pull the color outward with the roll of the flower. Also apply it under the ruffled edge of the open portion of the trumpet, where it overlaps the elongated section, and at the base of the trumpet next to the white petals. Touches may be added along the dips of the ruffled edge. Apply the color on a dry ground and then soften the blending edges with a damp, blotted filbert. This value should occupy less space than the first shading value.

Return to the outer petals and strengthen the shading color as needed. A stronger value of the original color is used. It should be applied on a dry ground. Soften the color edges slightly with a damp, blotted filbert. This stronger color is added to the deeper recesses of the white petals, where they rest under the trumpet or where two overlapping petals form a deep recess triangle.

Apply stronger touches of Oxide of Chromium to the predominant leaves. Apply the color to a dry ground with an appropriate-sized round sable brush. Soften with the damp, blotted filbert. Softer touches of Oxide of Chromium are also added to a few of the cooler leaves, to create a transition from the warmest, most predominant leaves to the coolest shadow leaves. Think of this color application as more of a stronger tint of color. It is not the shading color.

Apply pale color to the flower stem with Burnt Umber + a touch of Sepia + a touch of Oxide of Chromium. Base this in with an appropriate-sized round sable brush.

LEAF COLOR MIXES

Oxide of Chromium

Oxide of Chromium + Winsor Blue Red Shade + a touch of Sepia

Winsor Blue Red Shade + Sepia

15 Add an even stronger color to the flower trumpets with Gold Ochre + Permanent Alizarin Crimson + Burnt Umber. Apply this color to a dry ground, using the appropriate-sized round sable brush. Soften slightly with the damp, blotted filbert. Do not move this color out too far into the medium value area.

Apply pale warm tints to the outer petals with Burnt Umber + Sepia. Touch this color at the edges of the shaded areas as they are fading into the lighter areas. Apply the color with an appropriate-sized round sable brush to a dry ground. Soften the blending edges with a damp, blotted filbert.

On the front flower, apply very small touches of an even warmer tint near the lightest areas. Use a very pale value of Gold Ochre + Cadmium Yellow Pale, applied on a dry ground. Soften by skimming over the tint with a damp, blotted filbert.

Next, begin shading the leaves with a mixture of Oxide of Chromium + Winsor Blue Red Shade + Sepia. With an appropriate-sized round sable brush, apply to a dry ground and then soften with a damp, blotted filbert. Use this color in shadow point areas, where one leaf is behind another, or one portion of a leaf is behind another portion (such as a flipped or turned leaf). Also apply it along the vein and here and there on a leaf tip. Use it more strongly on the more predominant leaves. Use a softer shading value of the same mixture on the less predominant leaves.

Shade the flower stem with a stronger value of Burnt Umber + Sepia + Oxide of Chromium. Apply this under the flower and down the right side. Paint the color on a dry ground, then soften with a small, blotted filbert brush.

16 Add a final deep shading to the yellow trumpet areas with Permanent Alizarin Crimson + Burnt Umber. Apply the color to a very small area on a dry ground. Soften just slightly with the damp, blotted filbert brush.

Complete the shading on the leaves by adding a stronger shadow of Winsor Blue Red Shade + Sepia. Use this color in any deeper shadow point on the more predominant leaves, on the deep areas of the leaves formed by openings in the flower petals, to push the front leaves into the pitcher and as the final stem shading color. You may also use it in a softer value on less predominant leaves.

Complete the painting with various values of the Winsor Blue Red Shade + Sepia mixture. Use it in a stronger value for any additional strengthening in the background, pitcher, linen, white flower petals or leaves. Use this mixture to place the various elements in the atmosphere of the painting, by pulling it into any shadow point of one object that opens into a dark area of another element. Study the areas where the shadow points of the white petals open into dark areas of the background or leaves. You may also use strong values of this behind an element to pop it out or make it more predominant.

Use a softer value of the Winsor Blue Red Shade + Sepia mixture to wash over and subdue edges that are too bright or stark. Also add it as a cool tint to the yellow trumpet sections. Without these soft blue-gray tints, the yellow areas are too warm for the composition. As you begin to work with this color, you will continue to find places where it needs to be added in order to create depth and bring color harmony to your painting.

Finishing Your Project

The matting and framing of a watercolor composition can make or break a beautiful painting. Consider the mat as an extension of the composition—it should complement, but not overwhelm, the painting. The predominant outer mat I chose for this piece is pale cream. The narrower inside mats are soft taupe and a deep blue that repeats the blue china pattern hue. The deep blue was used directly next to the painting for accent and to aid in holding the eye of the viewer within the painting. See the framed painting on page 112.

Index